# Python Graphics

## Unleashing Creativity with Code

Williams Asiedu

# Python Graphics

*Unleashing Creativity with Code*



For permissions, inquiries, or licensing requests, please contact:
**Ouereila Publishing House**

**Email:** ouereila@gmail.com

**Forms:** ouereila?

**Ouereila Publishing House**
Python Graphics

**Author:** Williams Asiedu

# Python Graphics
# Unleashing Creativity with Code

```
>>> var = [2,6,4]
>>> sum(var)
12
>>> max(var)
6
```

# Table of Contents

# Preface

Being a programmer alone is not enough in a world where creativity and artistic design drive many industries. To truly stand out, you need to complement your coding skills with creativity. Python is a versatile language that spans multiple domains, including graphic design, which blends logic with visual aesthetics.

This book is your ultimate guide to leveraging Python for graphical design, image processing, and creative coding—all without the need for expensive graphic design software. With just your code, you can create stunning visuals and explore the artistic side of programming.

## Who This Book Is For

Whether in audio, eBook, or print format, this book is for anyone eager to master graphic design using Python. It goes beyond a simple introduction to Python, making it accessible even to beginners with little or no programming experience. Written in clear and straightforward English, it ensures an easy-to-follow learning experience for all.

## Structure of the Book

This book consists of nine chapters, each playing a crucial role in your journey as a graphic designer. If you already have Python programming skills, you can skip the earlier chapters and start directly with **Chapter 4: Python Graphics**.

*Chapter 1: Introduction to Programming*
This chapter introduces the fundamentals of programming, explaining its significance and the evolution of programming languages up to the present day.

*Chapter 2: Getting Started with Python*
Here, you'll learn about Python's origins, its syntax, and how to set it up on your system.

*Chapter 3: Python Programming Basics*
This chapter covers the core concepts of Python programming with numerous examples. If you are already familiar with Python, you may skip this chapter.

*Chapter 4: Introduction to Python Graphics*
This is where the main focus of the book begins. You'll be introduced to the essential modules and libraries for creating, designing, manipulating, editing, and processing images.

 

*Chapter 5: Image Processing with Pillow*
This chapter covers **Pillow**, a powerful library for image processing. You'll learn how to open, draw, filter, enhance, crop, rotate, recolor, and even create animations using Pillow's various modules.

*Chapter 6: Image Processing with OpenCV*
Here, you'll dive into **OpenCV**, learning how to process images using its extensive classes and functions for image design and manipulation.

*Chapter 7: ImageIO*
This chapter focuses on **ImageIO**, teaching you how to read, write, and convert images between different formats.

*Chapter 8: Drawing with Turtle Graphics*
In this chapter, you'll explore **Python's Turtle module** to create different shapes, figures, and visually appealing graphic designs.

*Chapter 9: About the Author*
The final chapter introduces the author, his work, and concluding remarks.

## Code Snippets
Each section of this book includes well-tested Python code snippets to help reinforce your learning. These examples allow you to understand concepts even without a physical device for practice.
Wishing you an exciting and creative coding journey! 🚀

 

```
C++
out<<"hello"<<endl;

Java
ystem.out.print("Hello");

C
rintf("hello");

JavaScript
onsole.Writline("hello");

PHP
cho "hello";
```

# INTRODUCTION TO COMPUTER PROGRAMMING

*After completing this chapter, you will be able to:*

- ☑ Define programming language.
- ☑ Understand the two types of programming languages.
- ☑ Know the various kinds of the programming languages.

# Introduction

Understanding the underlying mechanisms of computers and modes of communication has underscored the necessity for efficient programming. Today, programming permeates our daily lives, accessible to all without the need for formal certification. It has become an integral aspect of digital market dynamics, with software proliferation driving industry growth.

Programming languages serve as the cornerstone of software development, representing the gateway to becoming a programmer or app developer. Over the years, these languages have evolved significantly, transitioning from complex structures to user-friendly interfaces. This century's programming languages are notably more intuitive, facilitating easier comprehension and application in development processes.

Credit is due to the inventors of modern programming languages for their tireless efforts and contributions to software development. Their innovations have not only democratized programming but also empowered individuals from diverse backgrounds to participate in the digital economy.

## Programming Languages

Just as the name implies, language serves as a means of communication between two parties. Similarly, programming languages facilitate communication between users and computers through the use of symbols and objects, known as mnemonics. Since the inception of computers, programmers have continuously introduced new languages into the fold, each building upon or slightly altering the structure or syntax of its predecessors.

Programming languages are distinguished by their unique syntax, semantics, and intended applications. These languages range from low-level assembly languages, which directly interact with hardware, to high-level languages like Python and Java, which prioritize readability and ease of use. Despite their diversity, all programming languages share the common goal of enabling humans to instruct computers to perform specific tasks efficiently and accurately.

 

## How the Programming Languages work

The fundamental language of computers is binary code, consisting of sequences of ones (1) and zeroes (0). For example, the binary code 101 is interpreted by the computer as the digit 5. Known as machine language, this binary code is the sole language that computers inherently understand. However, communicating with computers through binary code directly is arduous and impractical for users.

To bridge this gap, programming languages are utilized to facilitate communication between users and computers. These languages are designed to be more human-readable and intuitive, allowing users to express instructions in a familiar syntax. When a user writes code in a high-level programming language, a special software called a compiler or interpreter translates this code into machine language that the computer can execute.

In essence, programming languages act as an intermediary, enabling users to convey instructions to computers in a more accessible manner, while compilers and interpreters serve as translators, converting these instructions into the binary code that computers comprehend. This process streamlines the programming workflow, making it feasible for individuals to develop software and interact with computers effectively.

## Kinds of Programming Languages

*Low-Level Programming Languages:*
Also known as machine language, low-level languages directly interact with hardware and consist of binary code represented by 0s and 1s. They are the most basic form of programming languages and are specific to the architecture of the computer's processor.

*High-Level Programming Languages:*
High-level languages are designed to be more user-friendly and abstracted from hardware specifics. They use natural language elements, symbols, and objects to make programming easier and more intuitive for humans. These languages are then compiled or interpreted into machine code.

| Language | Year | Origin | Inventor |
|---|---|---|---|
| Fortran | 1950 | - | IBM |
| Cobol | 1960 | - | Grace Hopper |

 

| | | | |
|---|---|---|---|
| Lisp | 1958 | - | John McCarthy |
| Pascal | 1970 | - | Niklaus Wirth |
| C | 1970 | BCPL | Denis Ritchie |
| C++ | 1980 | C | Bjarne Stroustrup |
| Perl | 1987 | C | Larry Wall |
| Python | 1991 | C, ABC | Guido Van Rossum |
| Java | 1991 | C | James Goslin (Oracle) |
| JavaScript | 1995 | ECMAScript | Netscape |
| C# | 2000 | Java, C++, Delphi | Anders Hejisberg |
| Kotlin | 2011 | Java | JetBrains |
| Dart | 2011 | C++ | Google |

*Table 1.0: High-Level Programming Languages*

 

# Chapter Summary

Programming is essential for software development and has become widely accessible, influencing various industries. Programming languages act as communication tools between humans and computers, evolving from complex structures to user-friendly formats.

Computers inherently understand only binary code (0s and 1s), but programming languages simplify interaction by allowing users to write instructions in a more readable format. These instructions are then translated into machine language using compilers or interpreters.

Programming languages are categorized into:

- Low-Level Languages (Machine Language & Assembly) – Directly interact with hardware.
- High-Level Languages (Python, Java, etc.) – Designed for ease of use and readability.

## Keywords

Compiler
Mnemonics
Interpreter
Binary

## Discussion

1. How do programming languages act as a bridge between humans and computers, and why is this necessary?

2. In what ways has the accessibility of programming changed the job market and opportunities in the digital economy?

3. What challenges do programmers face when transitioning from low-level to high-level programming languages?

4. Why is it important for new programming languages to be user-friendly, and how does this impact software development?

5. How do compilers and interpreters differ, and what role do they play in making programming languages functional?

# Review Questions

1. What is the primary purpose of programming languages?
   A) To design computer hardware
   B) To facilitate communication between humans and computers
   C) To replace operating systems
   D) To store data in binary format

2. Which of the following best describes machine language?
   A) A high-level programming language used in web development
   B) A language consisting of binary code (0s and 1s)
   C) A graphical interface for programming
   D) A language primarily used for database management

3. What role do compilers and interpreters play in programming?
   A) They directly execute binary code
   B) They convert programming code into machine language
   C) They manage computer memory
   D) They store programming syntax rules

4. Which of the following is a high-level programming language?
   A) Assembly
   B) Python
   C) Machine code
   D) Binary language

5. Why are high-level programming languages preferred over low-level languages?
   A) They execute faster than machine code
   B) They are more user-friendly and easier to learn
   C) They do not require a computer to run
   D) They eliminate the need for an operating system

6. What distinguishes low-level programming languages from high-level ones?
   A) Low-level languages use English-like syntax
   B) Low-level languages interact directly with computer hardware
   C) High-level languages do not require translation to machine code
   D) High-level languages only run on specific processor

7. What is the fundamental language that computers understand?
   A) Python
   B) JavaScript
   C) Binary code
   D) C++

8. How do modern programming languages contribute t the digital economy?
   A) By making programming accessible to more people
   B) By eliminating the need for developers
   C) By replacing hardware components
   D) By preventing cybersecurity threats

9. Why was there a need to develop high-level programming languages?
   A) To make coding more complex
   B) To allow humans to write instructions more intuitively
   C) To remove the need for operating systems
   D) To increase the processing power of computers

10. Which of these is NOT a characteristic of programming languages?
   A) Syntax and semantics
   B) Ability to interact with hardware
   C) A fixed structure that never evolves
   D) Being translated into machine code

```
ython

python –version
ython
>> import os
>> os.name
t'
>> os.mkdir("myfolder")
```

# STARTING PYTHON

*After completing this chapter, you will be able to:*

- ☑ List some importance of the Python language.
- ☑ Install Python on Windows, Linux and MacOS.
- ☑ Understand editors or IDEs.
- ☑ Use the Python IDLE.
- ☑ Use Visual Studio Code to run Python.
- ☑ Run Python scripts.
- ☑ Understand Python modules.

# Python

Python is a versatile and powerful programming language renowned for its readability, simplicity, and broad applicability across various domains. Developed by Guido Van Rossum in the late 1980s at the National Research Institute in the Netherlands, Python officially debuted in 1991. Since then, it has gained widespread adoption and popularity, becoming one of the most widely used programming languages globally.

Python's distinguishing features include being high-level, object-oriented, interactive, interpreted, and general-purpose. Its flexibility makes it suitable for a wide range of applications, including app development, data science, robotics, artificial intelligence, machine learning, web development, and game development.

One of Python's key strengths lies in its readability and simplicity. Python code is designed to resemble plain English, with keywords and syntax that are easy to understand and remember. This high-level scripting language allows developers to write concise and elegant code, facilitating rapid development and prototyping.

Moreover, Python boasts a vibrant and supportive community of developers and enthusiasts. This extensive community support ensures a wealth of resources, libraries, and frameworks readily available for developers to leverage in their projects, further enhancing Python's appeal and utility.

In essence, Python's combination of readability, versatility, and community support makes it an excellent choice for both beginners and experienced developers seeking to tackle a diverse range of programming challenges. Whether you're building web applications, analyzing data, or developing machine learning algorithms, Python offers the tools and resources necessary to bring your ideas to life effectively and efficiently.

## Installing Python

Python is an open-source programming language, which means it is free to use and modify. It can be freely downloaded from the Python software Foundation's website at https://www.python.org

 

## #Windows

Installing Python on Windows is indeed straightforward and hassle-free. Here's a concise guide:

1. Download Python: Visit the Python Software Foundation website (https://www.python.org/) and download the Python installer suitable for your Windows version.

2. Run the Installer: Once the download is complete, navigate to the location of the downloaded executable file (.exe) and double-click on it to launch the Python installer.

3. Installation Wizard: The installation wizard will guide you through the setup process. You can customize the installation by selecting optional features or changing the installation directory if desired.

4. Configure Environment Variables: During the installation process, ensure that you check the box labeled "Add Python to PATH." This option automatically configures the system environment variables to include the Python executable, making it accessible from any command prompt or PowerShell window.

*Figure : 2.0*

 

5. Complete Installation: Follow the prompts in the installation wizard to complete the installation process. Once the installation is finished, you can verify that Python is correctly installed by opening a command prompt and typing python --version. You should see the installed Python version displayed.

That's it! Python is now installed on your Windows system, and you're ready to start coding.

## *#Linux*

Indeed, Linux distributions often come with Python pre-installed. However, users may wish to install a different version or manage Python installations themselves. Here are the steps to install Python on Linux:

1. Update Package Lists: Open a terminal and update the package lists to ensure you have the latest information about available packages. Use the command:

```
sudo apt update
```

2. Install Python: Use the package manager to install Python. The package name might vary slightly depending on your distribution. For Python 3, you can use:

```
sudo apt install python3
```

3. Verify Installation: After the installation is complete, verify that Python is installed correctly by running:

```
Python3 --version
```

4. Optional: Install **pip** (Python Package Manager): Pip is a package manager for Python that allows you to install and manage additional libraries and packages. You can install pip using the following command:

```
sudo apt install python3-pip
```

 

That's it! You've successfully installed Python on your Linux system. You can now start using Python for development or other purposes.

## #MacOS

**1. Check Python Version (Optional):** macOS usually comes with a pre-installed version of Python 2.x. You can check the version by opening the Terminal and running:

```
python – -version
```

**2. Install Homebrew (Optional):** Homebrew is a package manager for macOS that simplifies the process of installing software. If you don't have Homebrew installed, you can do so by running the following command in Terminal:

```
/bin/bash -c "$(curl -fsSL
https://raw.githubusercontent.com/Homebrew/install/HEAD/install.sh)"
```

**3. Update Homebrew (Optional**): After installing Homebrew, it's a good idea to update it to ensure you have the latest version of available packages:

```
brew  update
```

**4. Install Python with Homebrew**: Use Homebrew to install Python by running the following command in Terminal:

```
brew install python
```

**5. Verify Installation**: After the installation is complete, verify that Python is installed correctly by running:

```
python --version
```

 

**6. Optional: Install pip (Python Package Manager):** If pip is not installed automatically, you can install it using the following command:

```
sudo easy_install pip
```

# Editors

Editors, or Integrated Development Environments (IDEs), are applications that enable users to write, edit, debug, and run programming code. They typically feature user-friendly interfaces with integrated tools, compilers, and debuggers tailored for specific languages. Some editors support multiple languages, while others are designed for a particular language.

Popular editors for Python development include:

- ✅ PyCharm
- ✅ Visual Studio Code
- ✅ Sublime Text
- ✅ Notepad++

Additionally, Python comes with its own integrated environment called IDLE. IDLE provides an interactive environment for writing and running Python code, making it particularly useful for practicing coding skills.

## Using IDLE

Using IDLE for Python coding is straightforward. Here's how to get started:

1. **Launch IDLE:**
   On Windows, open the Start menu and type "IDLE" to launch the IDLE editor.
   On Linux, open a terminal and type "idle" to launch IDLE.

 

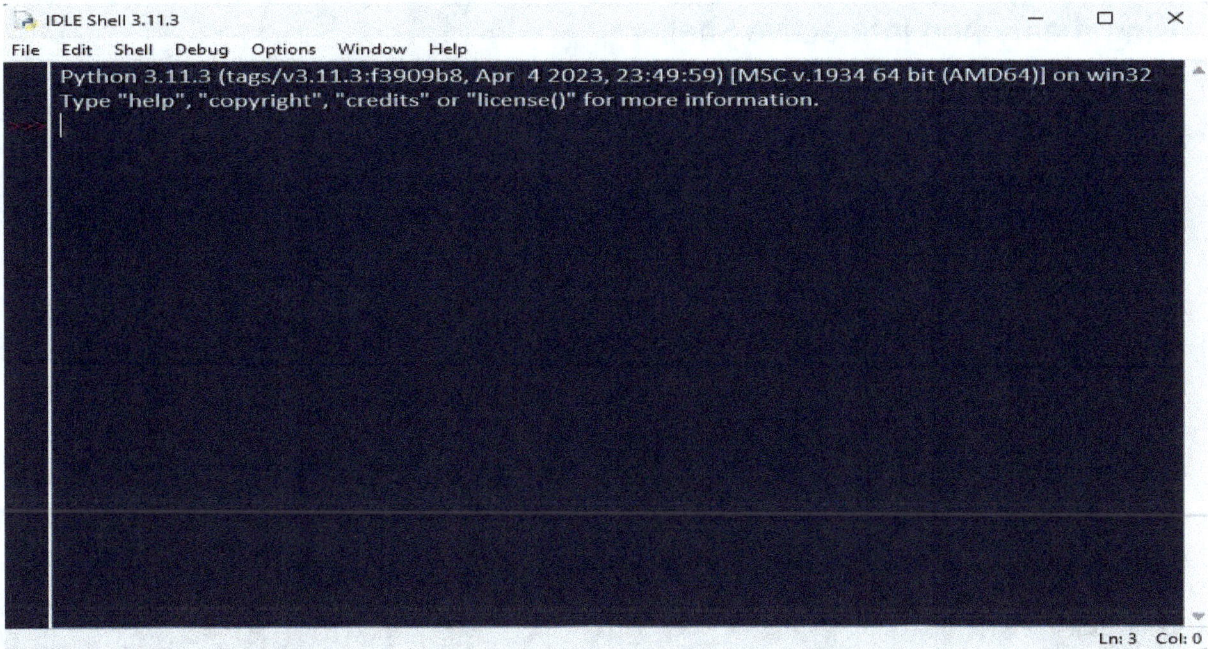


*Figure: 2.1*

**2. Create a New File:**
Once IDLE is open, click on the "File" menu and select "New File," or simply press Ctrl + N. This will open a new window where you can start writing your Python code.

**3. Write Your Code:**
Start writing your Python code in the new file window. You can use all the features of the IDLE editor, such as syntax highlighting and auto-indentation, to make coding easier.

**4. Run Your Code:**
After writing your code, you can run it by clicking on the "Run" menu and selecting "Run Module," or by pressing F5.
IDLE will execute your code and display the output in the interactive shell window.

Additionally, Python provides other interactive environments like IPython, which offers more advanced features and graphical capabilities for Python coding.

You can also use the native OS shell or command interface for simple Python coding tasks. This approach works the same way across all operating systems, including Windows, Linux, and macOS. Simply open a terminal or command prompt, type *"python"* to enter the Python interactive shell, and start coding directly in the shell environment.

 

## Using the Python Interactive Shell

1. Open the Command Line Interface (CLI):

   - On Windows, type "cmd" into the Windows search bar and press Enter to open the Command Prompt.
   - On Linux or macOS, open a terminal window.

2. Launch the Python Interactive Shell:

   - In the Command Prompt or terminal window, type "python" and press Enter.
   - This command starts the Python interpreter and opens the interactive shell, allowing you to enter Python code and receive immediate feedback.

```
C:\Users\Asiedu>python
Python 3.11.3 (tags/v3.11.3:f3909b8, Apr  4 2023, 23:49:59) [MSC v.1934 64 bit (AMD64)] on win32
Type "help", "copyright", "credits" or "license" for more information.
>>>
```

*Figure: 2.2*

That's it! You're now using the interactive Python shell, where you can experiment with Python code, test small snippets, and explore the language's features in real-time.

# Running Python

Running Python code can be accomplished through various methods and integrated development environments (IDEs) like PyCharm, Visual Studio Code, and IDLE. Here's a specific example using Visual Studio Code:

 

## The Visual Studio Code (VS Code)

VS Code is a versatile IDE developed by Microsoft, supporting numerous programming languages such as C, C++, Java, Python, C#, JavaScript, and HTML/CSS. It offers IntelliSense extensions to streamline programming tasks by providing suggestions for classes, functions, variables, and bug detection and correction. Additionally, VS Code is lightweight and features a user-friendly interface with buttons for running and debugging code.

### *#Windows*

1. Download VS Code:
   Visit the Visual Studio Code website or use the following link to download the VS Code executable file: *Visual Studio Code Download*.

2. Run the Installer:
   Once the download is complete, double-click on the downloaded executable file (usually named something like VSCodeSetup.exe) to run the installer.

3. Follow Installation Instructions:
   Follow the on-screen instructions provided by the installer to complete the installation process. You can choose installation options such as adding VS Code to the PATH and creating desktop shortcuts.

### *#Linux*

1. Download VS Code:

   On Linux, you can install Visual Studio Code using your distribution's package manager. For example, on Ubuntu, you can use the following commands in the terminal:

```
$ sudo apt update
$ sudo apt install code
```

 

### *#MacOS*

1. Download VS Code:
   Visit the Visual Studio Code website or use the following link to download the VS Code for macOS: *Visual Studio Code Download*.
2. Install VS Code:
   Once the download is complete, open the downloaded .dmg file.
   Drag the Visual Studio Code icon to the Applications folder to install VS Code on your macOS system.

After installing Visual Studio Code, you can launch it from the Start menu (Windows), applications menu (macOS), or by typing "code" in the terminal (Linux).

## Running Python code in Visual Studio Code

1. Install Python Extension (if not already installed):
   - ✓ Open Visual Studio Code.
   - ✓ Go to the Extensions view by clicking on the square icon on the sidebar or pressing Ctrl + Shift + X.
   - ✓ Search for "Python" or *"Pylance"* in the Extensions view and install the Python extension provided by Microsoft.

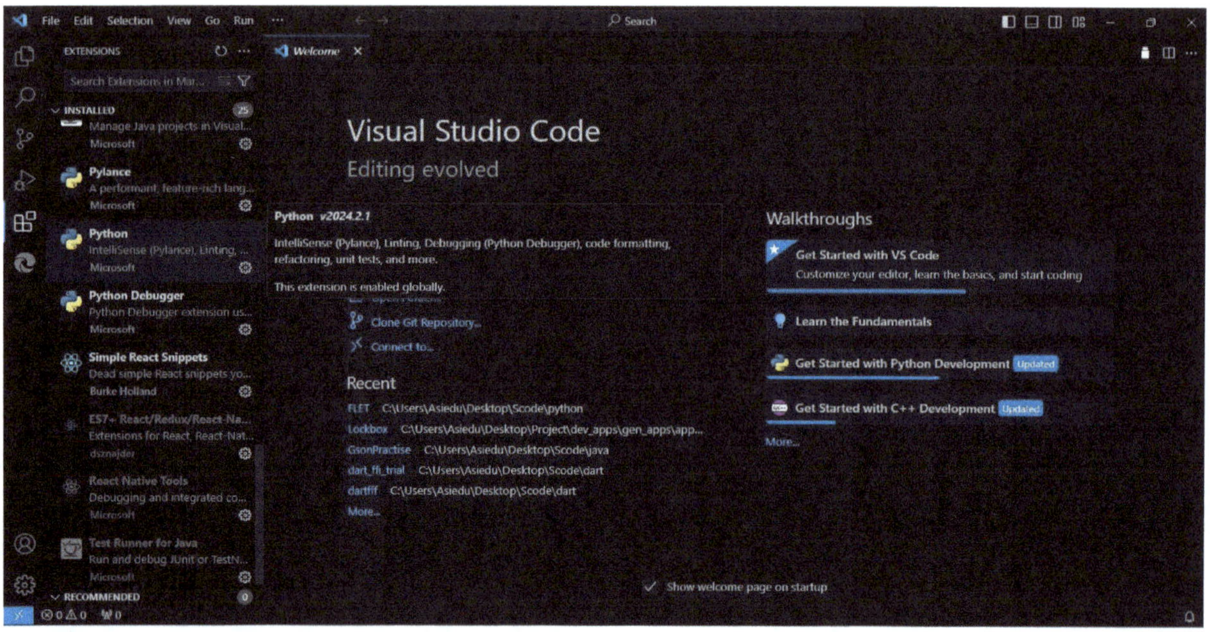


*Figure: 2.3*

 

2. Create or Open Python File:

   Create a new Python file or open an existing one in Visual Studio Code.
   - ✓ Click on the **"File"** menu at the top of the VS Code window.
   - ✓ Select **"New File"** to create a new file.
   - ✓ Name Your Python File:
     Type the preferred name of your Python file (e.g., "my_python.py").

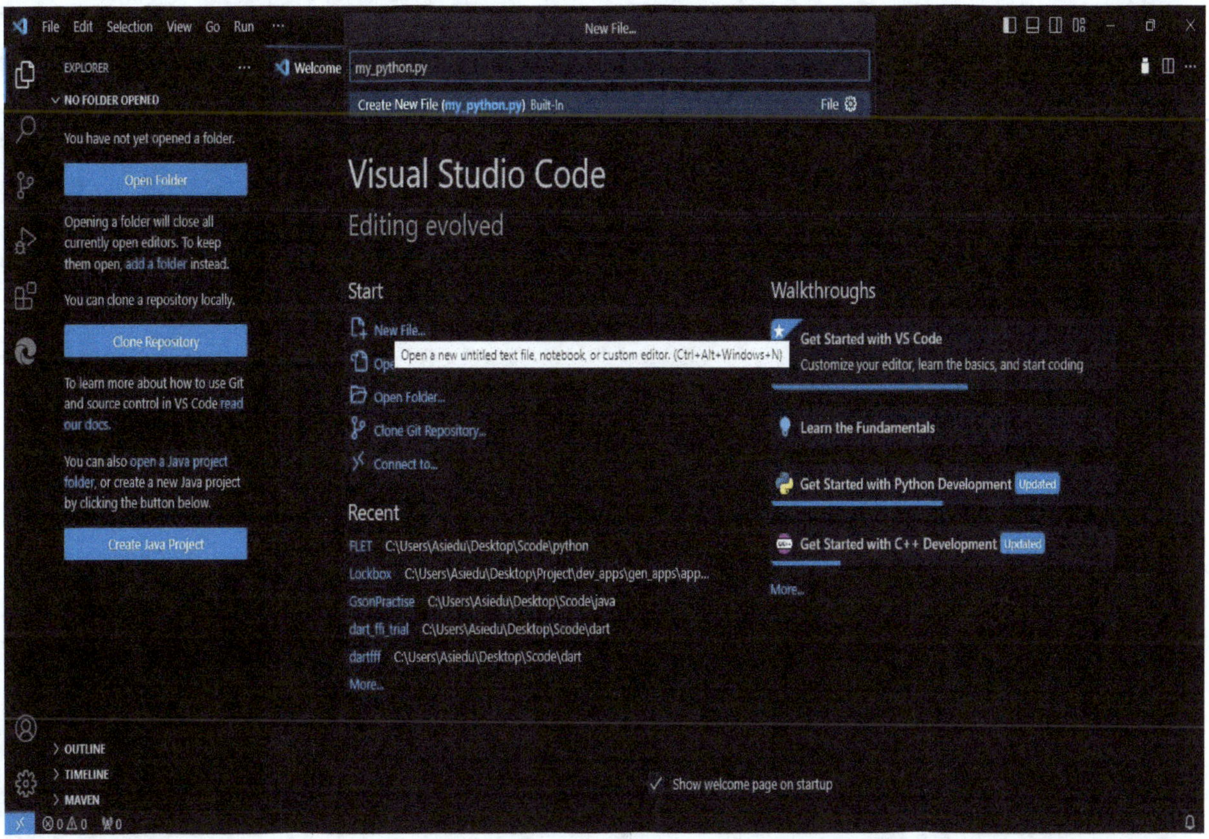


*Figure: 2.4*

3. Write Python Code:

   Write your Python code in the editor window. VS Code provides syntax highlighting and IntelliSense suggestions to assist you while coding.

 

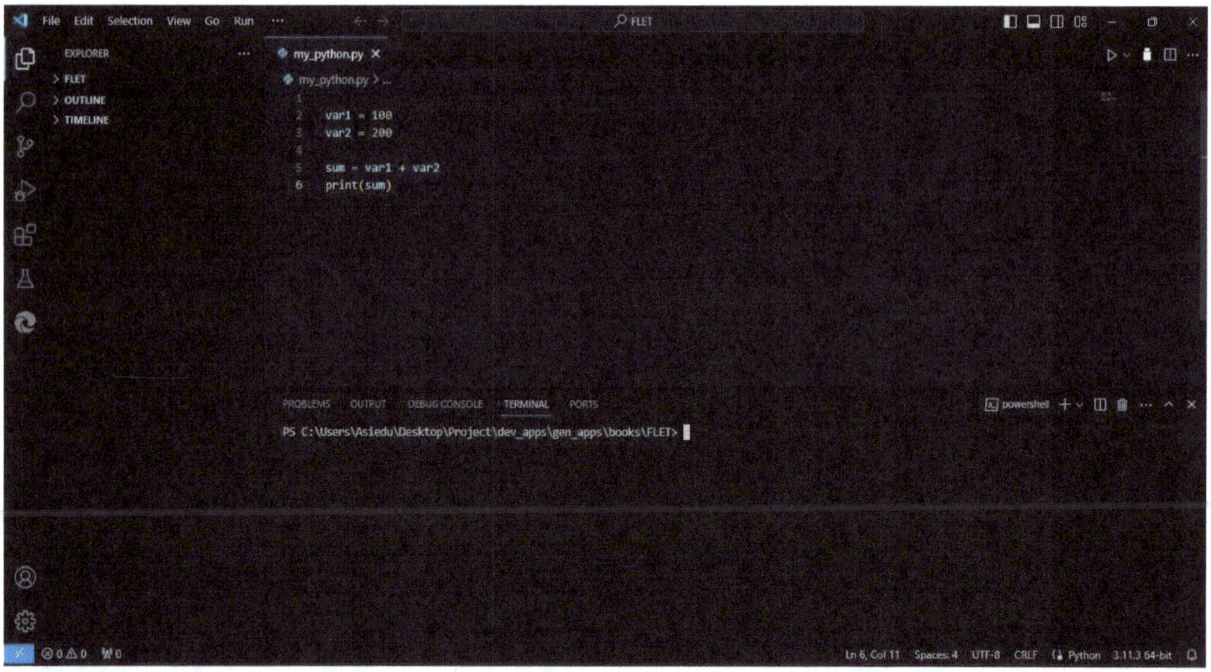

*Figure: 2.5*

4. Run Python Code:

   ✓ To run your Python code, you can use the Run button located in the toolbar at the top of the editor window. Alternatively, you can use the keyboard shortcut Ctrl + F5.

   VS Code will execute your Python code and display the output in the integrated terminal.

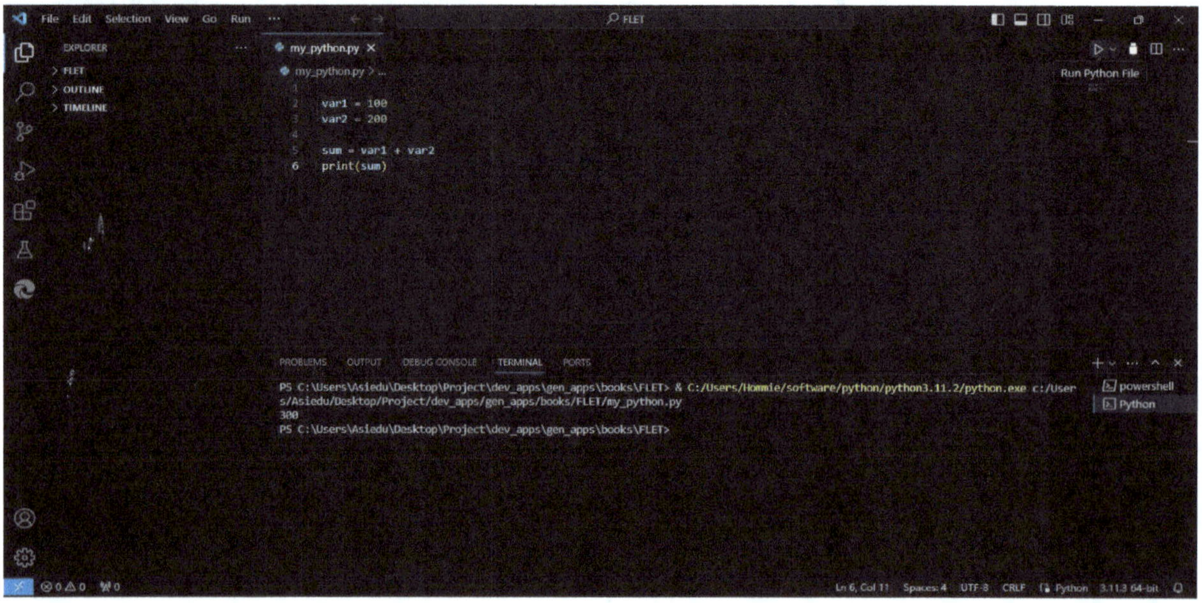

*Figure: 2.6*

 

## Executing Python from the Command Line

Running Python code from the command line or shell using the python command is a simple and universal approach that works across all operating systems, including Windows, Linux, and macOS.

Here's how you can run Python code from the command line:

*Open the Command Line or Terminal:*

1. On Windows, open the Command Prompt by searching for *"cmd"* in the Start menu.
2. On Linux or macOS, open the Terminal application.

*Navigate to the Directory Containing Your Python File (Optional):*

3. Use the **cd** command to navigate to the directory containing your Python file if it's not already there.

Run the Python File:

4. Type **python** followed by the name of your Python file and press the **Enter** key. For example: python my_script.py

```
PS C:\Users\Asiedu\Desktop\Project\dev_apps> python my_python.py
```

View Output (If Any):

If your Python script produces any output, such as printed messages or results, it will be displayed in the terminal after running the script.

This method provides a straightforward way to execute Python code directly from the command line or shell, making it convenient for quick tests or running scripts without the need for an integrated development environment (IDE) or text editor.

**Deep**

Python files are commonly recognized by their extension. **.py** for regular Python scripts or file and **.pyw** for scripts that run without displaying the console window.

 

# Modules or Libraries

Python modules are collections of code that provide additional functionality to Python programs. These modules are essentially Python files containing classes, functions and objects that can be imported and used in other Python scripts. They help simplify coding tasks by providing pre-defined solutions to common problems, thus saving developers time and effort.

While some modules are included in the Python standard library, many others are developed and maintained by the Python community. These external modules cover a wide range of domains and purposes, catering to diverse needs and preferences. For example, there are modules for web development, data analysis, machine learning, game development, and much more.

The beauty of Python modules lies in their versatility and flexibility. Developers can choose and install only the modules they need for their specific projects, allowing for a lightweight and efficient development process. For example, game developers may focus on installing modules essential for game development, while graphic designers may prefer using image processing libraries or modules to enhance their workflow.

Moreover, the open-source nature of Python encourages collaboration and contribution to module development, ensuring a rich ecosystem of tools and resources for Python programmers worldwide.

## Installing Python Modules with Pip

Installing Python modules is straightforward using the pip command, which is included as part of the Python package. Here's how you can install a Python module using pip on the command line or shell of any operating system:

1. Open the Command Line or Terminal:
2. Use the pip Command:

```
pip install module_name
```

Press Enter to execute the command.

 

For example, to install the NumPy module, you would type:

```
pip install numpy
```

Once the installation is complete, you can start using the module in your Python code. Using the module in your Python code is as simple as using the import keyword followed by the name of the module. For example

</> Python

```
>>> import numpy
>>>
```

This statement imports the specified module into your Python script, allowing you to use its classes, functions, and variables within your code.

**Note**

Import statement will be covered in more detail in later chapters.

**Deep**

Bugs, also known as errors, are issues in the code that prevent it from running correctly or producing the expected output. They can occur due to various reasons, such as logic error, semantic error, syntax error and runtime error.

 | 

## Chapter Summary

Python is a powerful and user-friendly programming language known for its readability, versatility, and ease of use. Created by Guido Van Rossum in the late 1980s and officially released in 1991, it has become one of the most popular languages worldwide.

Its key features include being high-level, object-oriented, and general-purpose, making it suitable for various applications such as web development, data science, artificial intelligence, machine learning, and game development. Python's simple syntax, resembling plain English, allows developers to write clean and efficient code, speeding up development and prototyping.

The language benefits from a vast community that provides extensive support, libraries, and frameworks making it even more accessible and adaptable. Developers can use popular editors like PyCharm, VS Code and Sublime Text, or Python's built-in IDLE. Additionally, Python modules expand functionality, offering pre built solutions for numerous tasks, from data analysis to game development.

Python can be executed through various methods, including integrated development environments or the command line, making it a flexible choice for developers across different platforms. Its open-source nature fosters collaboration, ensuring a continually evolving ecosystem of tools and resources.

### Keywords

| | | | |
|---|---|---|---|
| open-source | debugging | ipython | pylance |
| object-oriented | compilers | intellisense | class |
| function | object | import | syntax |
| runtime | semantic | | |

### Discussion

1. Why do you think Python has become one of the most popular programming languages worldwide?
2. How does Python's readability and simplicity contribute to its widespread adoption?
3. In what ways does Python's versatility make it suitable for various fields like AI, web development, and game development?
4. How does Python's open-source nature benefit developers and the programming community?
5. What are some advantages and disadvantages of using Python compared to other programming languages like Java or C++?
6. How does Python's extensive library support enhance its functionality for developers?
7. Why is community support important in the growth and development of a programming language like Python?
8. What role do Python modules play in simplifying programming tasks, and how do they contribute to efficient development?
9. How does Python's ability to run on multiple platforms (Windows, Linux, macOS) influence its usability?
10. What are some key considerations when choosing an IDE or editor for Python development?

# Review Questions

'ho developed Python?

ennis Ritchie
mes Gosling
uido van Rossum
jarne Stroustrup

which year was Python officially released?

985
991
000
008

hich of the following is NOT a key feature of
on?

igh-level
bject-oriented
ompiled
nterpreted

hat makes Python suitable for beginners?

omplex syntax
eadability and simplicity
mited functionality
ack of documentation

hich of the following is NOT a popular
ication of Python?

ata Science
'eb Development
perating System Development
rtificial Intelligence

6. Which of the following is an integrated development environment (IDE) for Python?

A) Notepad
B) PyCharm
C) Adobe Photoshop
D) Windows Explorer

7. What is the purpose of Python modules?

A) To execute system commands
B) To extend Python's functionality with reusable code
C) To compile Python programs into machine code
D) To make Python run faster

8. Which command is used to run a Python script from the command line?

A) run my_script.py
B) execute my_script.py
C) python my_script.py
D) start my_script.py

9. What is the name of Python's built-in interactive environment?

A) Jupyter Notebook
B) IDLE
C) Visual Studio Code
D) Terminal

10. Why is Python considered a general-purpose programming language?

A) It can only be used for a specific type of development
B) It is designed only for data science applications
C) It can be used for various applications like web development, AI, and game development
D) It only works on Windows systems

Chapter

```
#Python

>>> hex(10)
'0xa'
>>> sum([10,20,30)
60
>>> num= int(intput("num"))
num 10
>>> eval('10+20*8-4/1')
166.0
```

# OVERVIEW OF PYTHON

*After completing this chapter, you will be able to:*

Understand

- ☑ Variables and comment.
- ☑ Various reserved or keywords
- ☑ Operators
- ☑ Data types
- ☑ Numbers (integers and float)
- ☑ Strings and its methods
- ☑ List and its methods
- ☑ Dictionary
- ☑ Tuples
- ☑ Set
- ☑ Decision making statements
- ☑ Loops or control statements
- ☑ Functions
- ☑ Class and object
- ☑ Handling errors or exceptions

Quereila Publishing House

# Variable

Variable, also known as an identifier, is a term used to describe a letter or word that stores a value. Variables represent data stored in the computer's memory and can consist of any combination of letters, alphabets, or alphanumeric characters.

For example,

```
</> Python
>>> var = 100                #single value assignment
>>>
>>> var1, var2 = 2, 5        #multiple value assignment (var1 = 2, var2 = 5)
>>>
>>> x = y  = "computer"      #multiple value assignment (x = "computer", y = "computer")
```

In the above example:

- var is assigned to 100. Therefore, it holds a value of 100 in the computer memory.
- var1 and var2 are assigned to 2 and 5 respectively.
- x and y are assigned to the same value "computer".

## Rules for naming Variables

- Variables are case sensitive.
  *example:* myvar is not equal to Myvar.

- Variables cannot begin with a number but can be followed by numbers.
  *example*: myvar25, my63var.

- Variables can begin with underscores.
  *example:* _myvar

 

# Comment

Comments in programming serve as a means to document code, offer explanations, or add notes for better understanding. In Python, comments are not executed; rather, Python identifies them and skips their execution. Comments in Python are denoted by the '#' symbol.

For example:

**Python**

```
>>> num1 = 10  #first number
>>> num2 = 20  #second number
>>>
```

**Think about it ?**

Are any of these valid variables?

- xyz
- 45var
- myVar
- _6var1
- #num
- n@um
- --first

**Deep**

To check if an object is a valid variable name or identifier, use the .isidentifier() method on the string.

```
>>> "100var".isidentifier()
False
>>> "_var".isidentifier()
True
>>>
```

 

# Reserved Words

Python, like many programming languages, has a set of reserved keywords that serve specific purposes and functions within the language. These keywords are not available for use as variable names or for any other purpose in a Python program. Each reserved word carries a distinct and predefined functionality that is essential for the language's structure and operation.

| print | chr | hex | max | super | finally |
|---|---|---|---|---|---|
| len | else | range | raise | next | type |
| set | if | bin | sum | map | or |
| int | True | try | as | with | global |
| dict | False | eval | bool | while | local |
| list | and | not | str | for | catch |
| object | import | oct | ord | zip | super |
| exec | del | dir | any | def | return |
| len | hash | filter | format | enumerate | delattr |
| compile | bytearray | bytes | ascii | min | complex |
| id | local | help | in | open | lambda |

*Table 3.0: Some keywords used in Python programming*

For example,

### hex()

The hex keyword returns the hexadecimal of an integer or a number.

```python
>>> hex( 50 )
'0x32'
>>>
```

 

### bin()

The bin returns the binary of an integer or a number.

```
</> Python
>>> bin( 8 )
'0b1000'
>>>
```

### chr()

The chr function accepts an integer and returns its corresponding ASCII character.

```
</> Python
>>> chr( 65 )
'A'
>>> chr( 64 )
'@'
```

### ord()

The ord function accepts an ASCII character in a string and returns its corresponding integer.

```
</> Python
>>> ord( "B" )
66
>>> ord( "%" )
37
```

**Think about it ?**

What does the following functions return?

- eval()
- oct()
- id()
- ascii()
- dir()

 

# Operators

Operators are special symbols that appear between two operands (values or variables) and instruct the computer to perform specific operations. These operations can involve mathematical calculations, comparisons, assignments, and logical evaluations.

The various kinds of Python operators include:

- ✅ Arithmetic Operators
- ✅ Relational Operators
- ✅ Assignment Operators
- ✅ Logical Operators
- ✅ Identity Operators
- ✅ Membership Operators
- ✅ Bitwise Operators

## Arithmetic Operators

Arithmetic operators are used to perform various mathematical functions on numeric data types in programming. They enable you to perform fundamental mathematical operations like addition, subtraction, multiplication, division, and more.

### Addition( + )

</> Python

```
>>> x = 5
>>> y = 3
>>> result = x + y
>>> print( result )
8
>>>
```

 

## Subtraction( - )

```
</> Python
>>> x = 10
>>> y = 6
>>> result = x - y
>>> print( result )
4
>>>
```

## Multiplication( * )

```
</> Python
>>> num1 = 4
>>> num2 = 2
>>> product = num1 * num2
>>> print( product )
8
>>>
```

## Division( / )

```
</> Python
>>> first = 6
>>> second = 2
>>> first / second
3
>>>
```

## Modulo( % )

```
</> Python
>>> x = 3
>>> y = 11
>>> y % x
2
>>>
```

 

### Floor division( // )

```
</> Python
>>> x = 9
>>> y = 2
>>> x // y
4
>>>
```

### Exponential ( ** )

```
</> Python
>>> _exp = 2
>>> _num = 4
>>> _num ** _exp
16
>>>
```

## Relational Operators

Relational operators, also known as comparison operators, are essential components of conditional statements in Python. They are used to compare two values or operands and determine the relationship between them. Relational operators return a Boolean value, either **'True'** or **'False'**, based on the result of the comparison.

Relational operators are crucial for making decisions in programs. They help answer questions like "Is this value equal to that one?" or "Is this value greater than that one?"

```
</> Python
>>> "wheat" == "whaet"   #equal to
False
>>> "wheat" != "whaet"   #not equal to
True
>>> 4 < 10               #less than
True
>>> 5 > 3                #greater than
True
>>>
```

 

**Think about it ?**

- How is > different from **>=**?
- What about **<** and **<=**?

## Assignment Operators

Assignment operators serve the primary function of assigning a value on the right side to a variable on the left side. This assignment results in the variable holding the assigned value, thereby making it accessible for subsequent operations or references in your code. In Python, the most commonly used assignment operator is the equals sign (=), which assigns the value on the right side to the variable on the left side. For example:

**Python**

```
>>> x = 5
>>> name, age = "Alice", 20
>>> y = z = 10
>>>
```

Additionally, Python supports compound assignment operators, which combine an arithmetic operation with assignment. These operators include +=, -=, *=, /=, //=, %=, and **=, where the operator before the equals sign performs the specified operation on the variable and the value on the right side, and assigns the result back to the variable on the left side.

## Logical Operators

Logical operators are essential elements in Python used for making logical assumptions and decisions. They operate on Boolean values and return either 'True' or 'False' based on the logical conditions they evaluate. Logical operators are or, and, not. These operators are mostly used in decision making structures.

**Note**

Logical operators are mostly used in **if** clauses for making conditional statements or decision-making. This will be studied later under Decision making statements.

 

## Identity Operators

Identity operators in Python are tools used to verify or check whether two variables or objects are stored at the same memory location. They allow you to determine if two variables or objects refer to the same entity in memory, rather than comparing their values. Identity operators are essential for understanding object identity and reference equality. The two identity operators are is and is not.

```
</> Python
>>> m = n = 10
>>> x = 5
>>> m is n
True
>>> m is x
False
>>> m is not x
True
>>>
```

## Membership Operators

Membership operators in Python are tools used to check if a specific item is present in a collection of items. These operators are invaluable for determining whether an element belongs to a set, list, tuple, string, or any other iterable. They provide a straightforward way to search for the presence of an item within a container.

```
</> Python
>>> var = "computer"
>>> even = [2, 4, 6, 8]
>>> "com"  in var
True
>>> "z"  in var
False
>>> 5 not in even
True
>>>
```

 

# Data Types

Data encompasses raw values that can manifest in various forms, such as numbers, letters, special characters or a blend thereof. Data types serve to classify data based on their attributes and functionalities.

In Python, data types represent instances or objects of specific classes, each characterized by unique traits and behaviors. The Python programming language encompasses approximately eight fundamental data types. The various types of data types in Python include:

- Numbers (Integer and Float)
- String
- List
- Dictionary
- Tuple
- Set
- Boolean
- Bytes

**Deep**

To check the data type of an object, use the type() function.

```
>>> var = 3
>>> type(var)
class <'int'>
>>>
```

 

# Numbers

## Integer

The integer class encompasses all numbers, including negative numbers, without decimal points. The int() function is employed to convert from one type to the integer type. Example: 2, 13, -5, 100, 2000 ......

## Float

On the other hand, floats represent the class of all numbers with decimal points. To convert from one type to the float type, the float() function is utilized. Example: -6.25, 8.5245, -5.3, 100.6 ......

Some methods used with the number type

```
</> Python
>>> import math
>>> m , n = 5, 2
>>> var = 0.47
>>> pow( m, n )                    #exponential function
25
>>> math.sqrt( 16 )                #square root function
4.0
>>> math.log( 10 )                 #logarithm function
2.302585092994046
>>> math.ceil( var )               #rounds a number up to the next largest whole number
1
>>> math.cos( var )                #cosine function
0.891568288195329
>>> math.round( 20.58952, 3 )      #rounds to a number of decimal places
20.59
>>>
```

**Deep**

The math() function is one of Python modules used to perform various mathematical functions. You can explore more methods of math with the dir() function.

```
>>> import math
>>> dir(math)
[...........]
```

 

# String

A string is a sequence of characters, including alphabets, numbers, or special characters, enclosed within quotes. String can be in a single or double quote.

For example,

</> **Python**

```
>>> var1 = 'single'
>>> var2 = "double"
>>> var3 = '''triple'''
>>> var4 = """triple"""
```

**Deep**

The str() method is used to convert other data types to a string.

```
>>> var = 3.45
>>> string_var = str(var)
>>> print(string_var)
'3.45'
>>>
```

## String indexing

Indexing refers to the position of each character in a string. The index of a string starts from zero and goes up to the length of the string minus one (0 to length-1). The first character or element of a string typically occupies index 0, the next character takes index 1, and so on.

For example,

</> **Python**

```
>>> var = "computer"
>>> var[0]
'c'
>>> var[1]
'o'
>>> var[7]
'r'
>>>
```

 

## Concatenating string

Concatenating strings involves adding two or more separate strings to form one complete string using the plus (+) operator.

For example,

```
</> Python
>>> var1 = "com"
>>> var2 = "puter"
>>> var3 = var1 + var2
>>> print(var3)
'computer'
>>>
```

## Slicing a string

String slicing allows you to extract substrings from a string. The syntax for string slicing is **string**[start : end], where start indicates where the slicing should begin and end indicates where it should end. Both start and end parameters can be omitted, in which case Python will set them to default values (0 for start and the last index of the string for end).

```
</> Python
>>> var = "Hello World"
>>> var[0:5]                #start = 0, end=5
'Hello'
>>> var[6:]                 #start = 6, end= length of string
'World'
>>> var[:3]                 #start = 0, end=3
'Hel'
>>> var[1:5]                #start = 1, end=5
'ello'
>>>
```

 

## Some methods used with the string type

len() and count()

```
</> Python
>>> string1 = “computer”
>>> len(string1)                #length of the string
8
>>> var = “programming”
>>> var.count( ’m’ )            #returns the number of times a character appears in string
2
```

index() , ridex() , find() and rfind()

```
</> Python
>>> var = “programming”
>>>var.index( ’g’ )             #returns the first occurrence of a character
3
>>>var.rindex( ’r’ )            #returns the last occurrence of  a character
4
>>> var[4]                      #returns the index of a character
’r’
>>> var.find( ’m’ )             #returns the first occurrence of a character
6
>>> var.rfind( ’m’ )            #returns the last occurrence of  a character
7
```

replace()

```
</> Python
>>> cat = “brown cat”
>>> cat.replace( "cat", ‘fox’ )   #substitutes all occurrences of old value with new value
’brown fox’
>>>
```

upper(), lower(), capitalize() and title()

```
</> Python
>>> com = “computer”
>>> com.upper( )                #converts all letters in a string to uppercase
’COMPUTER’
>>> com.capitalize( )           #makes the first letter uppercase and the rest lowercase
’Computer’
```

 

```
>>> mystr = "Python is great!"
>>> mystr.lower( )                #converts all letters in a string to lowercase
'python is great!'
>>>com.islower()                  #returns True if every letter is lowercase, otherwise False.
True
>>>mystr.title()                  #Capitalizes the first letter of each word.
'Python Is Great!'
>>>mystr.isupper()                #returns True if every letter is uppercase, otherwise False.
False
>>> mystr.istitle()   #returns True if the first letter of each word is uppercase, otherwise False
False
>>>
```

split()

```
</> Python
>>> str1 = "I love programming"
>>> str2 = "coding + coffee -> great coding"
>>> str1.split( )                 #break string into list of words based on white spaces - default
['i', 'love', 'programming']
>>> str1.split( maxsplit=1 )                #maximum string division is one
['i', 'love programming']
>>> str2.split( sep='+' )                   #break string into list of words based on "+"
['coding ', ' coffee - great coding']
>>> str2.split( sep='->' )
['coding + coffee ', ' great coding']
>>>
```

isnumeric() , isalpha() and isalnum()

```
</> Python
>>> num = "1234"
>>> lett = "abcd"
>>> lettnum = "abcd1234"
>>> num.isnumeric( )          #returns True if every character is a number; otherwise False
True
>>> lett.isalpha( )           #returns True if every character is a letter; otherwise False
True
>>> lettnum.isalnum( )   #returns True if every character is a letter or a number; otherwise
True                     #False
>>> lettnum.isnumeric( )
False
>>>
```

 

# List

A list is a collection of items of the same type or different types, enclosed in square brackets [ ]. Lists perform functions similar to arrays in C, C++, and Java. They can contain other lists, making them a preferred choice for storing large data of different types.

```
</> Python
>>> even = [2, 4, 6, 8, 10]                                                  #list of numbers
>>> items = ["mouse", "keyboard", "microphone"]                              #list of string
>>> mix = [ 5, "mouse", 4.25, ('age', 30), {'name' : "John"}, [2, 4] ]       #list of different types
>>>
```

**Note**
The first element of a list occupies index **0**, the next at index **1** and so on.

## Slicing a list

Lists can be divided to obtain sub-lists using slicing notation list[start : end]. The start parameter is optional and specifies where the division should begin. If start is not set, Python begins the division from the first element (index 0). Similarly, the end parameter is optional. If not specified, Python sets it to the last index of the list. For example:

```
</> Python
>>> num = [2, 5, 1, 8]
>>> mum[1:3]                #start = 1, end = 3
[5, 1]
>>> num[1:]                 #start = 1, end = length of list -1
[5, 1, 8]
>>> num[:2]                 #start = 0, end = 2
[2, 5]
>>>
```

**Deep**
The list() function is used for converting other data types to list.

```
>>> list("programming")
['p', 'r', 'o', 'g', 'r', 'a', 'm', 'm', 'i', 'n', 'g']
>>>
```

 

## Some methods used with list

count()

```python
>>> students = [ 'Alice ', 'Bob ', 'John ', 'Ben ', 'John ' ]
>>>
>>> students.count('Alice ')          #It returns the number of occurrences of a member
1
>>> students.count('John')
2
```

append() , extend() and insert()

```python
>>> even = [2, 4, 6]
>>> odd = [1, 3, 5]
>>>
>>> even.extend( odd )       #adds a list to form a single list
>>> even
[2, 4, 6, 1, 3, 5]
>>> odd.append( 7 )          #adds an item to the list
>>> odd
[1, 3, 5, 7]
>>> odd.insert( 2, 9 )       #inserts item at a specified index
>>> odd
[1, 3, 9, 5, 7]
>>>
```

pop() , remove() and clear()

```python
>>> var = [1, 2, 3, 4]
>>>
>>> var.remove( 2 )         #removes an item from the list
>>> var
[1, 3, 4]
>>> var.pop( )              #deletes the last item from the list
>>> var
[1, 3]
>>> var.clear( )            #deletes all items and returns an empty list
>>> var
[ ]
>>>
```

 

reverse() and sort()

```
</> Python
>>> letters = [ 'b', 'd', 'a', 'c' ]
>>>
>>> letters.sort( )              #It arranges members in ascending order by default
>>> letters
['a', 'b', 'c', 'd']
>>> letters.reverse( )           #It changes the direction of its members.
>>> letters
['d', 'c', 'b', 'a']
>>>
```

sum() , max() and min()

```
</> Python
>>> num = [1, 6, 4, 3]
>>>
>>> sum( num )        #returns the summation of list members
14
>>> min( num )        #returns the smallest value or member of the list
1
>>> max( num )        #returns the largest  value or member of the list
6
>>>
```

**Think about it ?**

Does **copy()** actually create a copy of a list, as its name suggest?

 

# Tuple

Tuples are collections of elements of different data types enclosed in parentheses ( ) and separated by commas. The elements of tuples are immutable, meaning they cannot be changed once created, but they can still be accessed.

For example,

```
</> Python
>>> tup1 = (3, 4, 2)                                              #tuple of numbers
>>> tup2 = ("Python", "Java",  "C++")                             #tuple of strings
>>> tup3 = (5, 3.25, ('id', 30), "Texas", {'name' : "Alice"}, [6, 2] )   #tuple of different types
>>>
```

**Deep**

The tuple() function is used to convert other data types to tuple.

```
>>> var = ("code")
>>> tuple(var)
('c', 'o', 'd', 'e')
>>>
```

## Some methods used with tuple

count()

```
</> Python
>>> tup = ( 1, 2, 2, 5, 1, 2 )
>>>
>>> tup.count( 1 )
2
>>> tup.count( 2 )
3
>>>
```

 

index()

```
</> Python
>>> even = ( 4, 6, 2)
>>> even.index(4 )
0
>>> even.index( 2 )
2
>>> group = ( (2, 4), (1, 0.3, ["Texas", "London"]), (5, "Alice") )
>>> group[ 2 ]
 (5, 'Alice')
>>> group[ 2 ] [ 1 ]
 'Alice'
>>>
```

sum() , max() and min()

```
</> Python
>>> num = (2, 5, 3)
>>>
>>> sum( num )        #returns the summation of tuple numerical  members
10
>>> min( num )        #returns the smallest value or member of the tuple
2
>>> max( num )        #returns the largest  value or member of the tuple
5
>>>
```

 

# Dictionary

A dictionary is a data structure that consists of a collection of key-value pair items, separated by commas, and enclosed within curly braces { }. Dictionaries can contain items of various data types. In a key-value pair, one item (the key) is associated with another item (the value), and they are linked by a colon (key : value).

For example,

Python

```
>>> dic1 = {'name' : "Alice", 'age' : 20, 'country' : "USA"}
>>> dic2 = {'numbers' : [2, 4],  'languages' : ("Python", "Java") }
>>> dic3 = { 1 : 100,  2 : 200,  3 : 300}
>>>
```

Deep

The dict() function is used to convert other data types (tuple) to dictionary.

```
>>> var = ( ("name", "John"), ("ID", 250), ("city", "London") )
>>> dict(var)
{'name': 'John', 'ID': 250, 'city': 'London'}
>>>
```

## Some methods used with dictionary

get() and dictionary[key]

Python

```
>>> student = { 'fname' : 'George', 'lname' : 'Wood', 'college' : 'MIT', 'index' : 1540 }
>>>
>>> student.get( 'fname' )
'George'
>>> student.get( 'index' )
1540
>>> student[ 'college']
 'MIT'
>>>
```

 

update()

```
</> Python
>>> fruits = { 1 : "mango", 2 : "apple",  3 : "grape",  4 : "banana",   }
>>>
>>> fruits[ 3]  = "orange"
>>>
>>> print( fruits)
{1: 'mango', 2: 'apple', 3: 'orange', 4: 'banana'}
>>>
>>> fruits.update( {2 : "berry"})
>>> fruits
{1: 'mango', 2: 'berry', 3: 'orange', 4: 'banana'}
>>>
```

pop()

```
</> Python
>>> city = { "USA" :  "New York ",  "England" : "London",  "Canada" : "Toronto" }
>>>
>>> city.pop('England')
'London'
>>> city
{'USA': 'New York', 'Canada': 'Toronto'}
>>>
```

keys() and values()

```
</> Python
>>> profile = { 'college' : 'Harvard',  'course' : 'Computer Science', 'index' : 10048 }
>>>
>>> profile.keys( )
dict_keys(['college', 'course', 'index'])
>>>
>>> profile.values( )
dict_values(['Harvard', 'Computer Science', 10048])
>>>
```

 

# Set

A set is an unordered collection of unique elements. Sets enclose their members within curly braces { }. Sets can hold members of strings, integers, floats, and tuples, but not dictionaries, lists, or other sets. Sets are commonly used to perform mathematical operations such as intersection, union, or symmetric difference.

For example,

</> **Python**

```
>>> set1 = {1, 3, 5, 7}
>>> set2 = {2, 4, 6, "orange", "apple" }
>>>
```

**Deep**

The set() function is used to convert other data types to set.

```
>>> list_var = [2, 3, 5]
>>> set(list_var)
{2, 3, 5}
>>>
```

## Some methods used with dictionary

add() , remove(), and discard()

</> **Python**

```
>>> var = {1, 3, 6}
>>>
>>> var.add(9 )
>>> var
{1, 3, 6, 9}
>>> var.remove(6)
>>> var
{1, 3, 9}
>>> var.discard(1)
>>> var
{3, 9}
>>>
```

 

union(), intersection() and difference()

```python
>>> set1 = {1, 3, 5, 6}
>>> set2 = {2, 3, 4, 5}
>>>
>>> set1.union( set2 )          #returns a set containing all unique elements from both sets
{1, 2, 3, 4, 5, 6}
>>> set1.intersection( set2 )  #returns a set containing common elements of both sets
{3, 5}
>>> set1.difference( set2 )    #returns a set containing elements that are in the first set but
{1, 6}                          #not in the second set
>>>
```

Isdisjoint(), issubset() and issuperset()

```python
>>> U = {1, 2, 3, 4, 5, 6}
>>> var = {1, 3, 4, 6}
>>> U.issuperset( var )    #returns True if the set contains all elements of the given set
True
>>> var.issubset( U )      #returns True if all elements of the set are present in the other set
True
>>> U.isdisjoint( var )    #returns True if the two sets have no common elements
False
>>>
```

sum() , max() and min()

```python
>>> num = {2, 3, 5, 6}
>>>
>>> sum( num )       #returns the summation of the set  members
16
>>> min( num )       #returns the smallest value or element of the set
2
>>> max( num )       #returns the largest  value or element of the set
6
>>>
```

 

# Decision Making

Decision making is crucial in programming, especially when you want your program to execute only when a certain condition is true or false. These statements, known as conditional statements, are based on a Boolean value (True or False). There are three different kinds of conditional statements:

## 1. if Statement:

This is a simple conditional statement that executes a program or instructions if a condition is true or false

</> Python

```
if condition:
  #code
```

For example,

A program to print "Hello World!" when variable is equal to 5.

</> Python

```
if var == 5:
  print("Hello World!")
```

## 2. if – else Statement:

The if-else conditional statement provides two options for program execution. If the given condition is true, the program executes the statements in the if block; otherwise, if the condition is false, the statements within the else block execute.

</> Python

```
if condition:
  #code
else :
  #code
```

 

For example:

A program to print "Great Python", if a variable is greater than 5, otherwise print "Awesome Python".

```
</> Python
var = 4
if  var > 5:
    print("Great Python!")
else:
    print("Awesome Python!")
```

## 2. if – elif – else Statement:

This conditional statement is necessary for multiple decision making

```
</> Python
if condition1:
  #code
elif condition2:
  #code
elif condition3:
  #code
.......
.......
else :
  #code
```

 

For example:

A program to print "great Python!", if a variable is equal to 5. If it is greater than 5, print "awesome Python"; otherwise print 'good Python'.

</> **Python**

```
var = 3
if   var == 5:
     print("Great Python!")

elif var < 5:
     print("Awesome Python")

else :
     print("Good Python")
```

 

# Loops

A loop is a control structure that enables the repetitive execution of a statement or a group of statements. Loops are built around conditions, steps, and statements. They keep executing as long as the condition is true. There are two kinds of loop structures in Python: for and while.

## The for loop

The for loop is a control structure that allows the repetitive execution of statements in a top-to-bottom approach. It is used to iterate over elements of sequential data types such as lists, strings, or tuples.

</> Python

```
for item in iterable:
    #code
```

**Note**

Iterable is an object capable of returning its members one at a time. It can be traversed or looped over using **for** loops. Examples include list, tuple, string, dictionary and set.

For example,

</> Python

```
string_var = "code"

for  item in string_var:
     print(item)
......
c
o
d
e
```

 

```python
list_var = [1, 2, 3, 4]

for  item in list_var:
      print(item)
.....
1
2
3
4
```

**Note**

- Indentation is crucial in **for** and **while** loops.
- Every **for** or **while** statement must end with a colon (:).

# Range

Loop structures execute code based on user-given instructions, specifying where to begin, end, and the steps. These instructions can be easily implemented using the *range()* function.

The **range(** start, end, step**)** function is used to specify the range of values and steps a control structure must follow to execute the program. The *start* parameter is optional and denotes where to begin the loop. It is set to **0** by default. The *end* parameter must always be specified and denotes the integer to end the loop. The *step* is also an optional parameter that specifies the interval of execution. It is set to **1** by default.

 

For example,

range(end)

```
</> Python

for i in range( 4 ):      #end = 4
    print( i )
.....
0
1
2
3
```

range(start, end)

```
</> Python

for i in range( 2, 6 ):      #start = 2  end = 6
    print( i )
.....
2
3
4
5
```

range(start, end, step)

```
</> Python

for i in range( 0, 10, 2 ):      #start = 0  end = 10  step=2
    print( i )
.....
0
2
4
6
8
```

 

## The while loop

The while loop is another control structure used to iterate or repeatedly execute a set of statements based on a true condition. The loop terminates when the condition is no longer true.

```
</> Python
while condition:
    #code
```

For example,

```
</> Python
i = 0
while i < 4:        #repeat iteration until i = 4  (condition becomes false or no longer true)
....    i = i + 1       #increment i by one in each iteration
....    print( i + 2 )
....
3
4
5
6
```

**Deep**

To create an infinite loop, set the condition to always be True and terminate with Ctrl + C.
Infinite loop:

```
while True:
    print("Hello World!")
.....
.....
```

**Think about it ?**

Did the loop run forever using the True condition? How true is that? Infinite loops can gradually consume system resources, degrading performance. You can interrupt the iteration using Ctrl + C.

 

## The break statement

The break statement is a Python keyword used mostly in loop structures to halt or terminate execution prematurely once a given condition is true.

For example,

```
</> Python

for  i in range( 1, 5 ):
      if  i == 3:            #terminate loop once i = 3
         break
      print( i )
.....
1
2
```

## The continue statement

The continue statement is also a Python keyword implemented in loops to skip a step or iteration when a particular condition is true.

For example,

```
</> Python

for  i in range( 1, 6 ):
      if  i == 3:            #skip step 3
         continue
      print( i )
.....
1
2
4
5
```

 

# Function

A function is a block of organized and related statements used to perform a specific task. It can contain variables, loops, decision-making statements, other functions, statements, and objects that can be used repeatedly in different parts of a program. Functions are also referred to as methods, procedures, subprograms, routines, or subroutines.

## Importance of Functions:

- ☑ Enhanced Readability and Comprehensibility:

Functions improve the readability and comprehensibility of a program by breaking it down into smaller, logical units. Each function performs a specific task, making the code easier to understand.

- ☑ Efficiency through Minimization of Repetitions:

Functions help minimize repetitions in code by encapsulating repetitive tasks into reusable blocks. This reduces the amount of code duplication and makes the program more efficient to maintain.

- ☑ Breaking Complex Programs into Smaller Segments:

Functions allow complex programs to be broken down into smaller and more manageable segments. Each function focuses on a specific aspect of the program's functionality, making it easier to develop and debug.

- ☑ Improved Time Efficiency:

By organizing code into functions, developers can optimize performance and improve time efficiency. Functions enable code reuse, which reduces development time and effort, leading to faster and more efficient programming.

 

## Types of Functions in Python:

There are two types of functions in the Python programming language: Built-in Functions and User-defined Functions.

### Built-in Functions:

Built-in functions are provided by the Python language and are readily available to be used in programs. They serve various purposes and are commonly used for tasks such as mathematical operations, data conversion, string manipulation, and more.

Examples include: sum(), eval(), hex(), bin(), oct(), chr(), ord(), dir(), del(), max(), min(), len()

Example of using built-in functions

```
</> Python
>>> var = [2, 4, 6]
>>> total = sum( var )
>>> print( total )
12
>>>
```

### User-defined Functions:

User-defined functions are functions created by the user according to Python syntax. These functions allow developers to encapsulate specific tasks or operations into reusable blocks of code, enhancing code modularity and reusability.

Syntax

```
</> Python

def function_name(param):
    #statement

    return  #statement
```

 

✏️ The def Keyword:
The def keyword is used to define a function in Python. It is the keyword used to create a function.

✏️ Function Name:
The function name is the identifier given to the function. It can start with either a capital or lowercase letter and can include underscores, but it cannot start with a number.

✏️ Parameters:
Parameters, also known as arguments, are optional and used to pass data or values to the function. They are specified within the parentheses following the function name.

✏️ Colon:
A colon (:) marks the end of the function header, indicating the start of the function block or body.

✏️ Statement(s):
Every function block or body contains at least one statement, which defines the actual logic or purpose of the function. These statements are executed when the function is called.

✏️ The return Statement:
The return keyword is optional and is used if the function is defined to return or produce a value. If the function is designed to return no value, there is no need to use the return statement.

Example 1: A function to print "Hello World!"

</> Python

```python
def hello( ):
    print( "Hello World!" )
```

Example 2: A function to accept two numbers and return their sum

</> Python

```python
def total( x, y ):
    result = x + y

    return result
```

 

## Calling Functions:

Calling a function simply means executing the function. Function calls can be made through the Python prompt, within another function, or within a program.

Example 1,

```
</> Python

>>> def greetings( name ):
        print( f" hello  {name}" )
.....
.....
>>> greetings( "Alice" )    #calling the greetings function
hello Alice
>>>
```

Example 2

```
</> Python

def total( x, y ):
    result = x + y
    return result

def largest( *args ):
    large = max( args )
    return large


result = total( 10, 20 )            #calling the total function
print( result )                     #output:  30

value = largest( 1, 5, 12, 6)       #calling the largest function
print( value )                      #output:  12
```

 

## Anonymous Function

Python functions are normally defined with the def keyword, but there is another way to create functions without using the def keyword and a function name. This can be achieved using Python Lambda functions.

Syntax

```python
>>> variable = lambda arguments : expression
```

- **Variable:** This is the variable that will store the lambda function.
- **Argument:** These are the input values provided to the lambda function.
- **Expression:** This is the logic that defines the function.

Example 1 : Lambda function to add two numbers.

```python
>>> add = lambda x , y : x + y
>>> add( 2, 5)
7
>>>
```

Example 2 : Lambda function to return the square of a number.

```python
>>> square = lambda x  : x ** 2
>>> square( 4 )
16
>>>
```

Example 3 : Lambda function to check if a number is even.

```python
>>> even = lambda x  : x % 2 == 0
>>> even( 6 )
True
>>>
```

 

# Class and Object

Python is a purely object-oriented programming (OOP) language where everything is an object. A class is a data type, similar to built-in types like list, string, dictionary, float, or integer.

An object, on the other hand, is an instance of a class and can be any named entity, such as functions, integers, strings, floats, classes, methods, and files.

Objects are created from classes, and each object is called an instance of a class. Classes can have functions or variables, where functions defined in a class are called methods and variables are called class attributes.

Example:

```python
class Myclass:                  #class name
    num = 10                    #class attribute (variable)
    name = "Bob"

    def greetings():            #class method (function)
        value = f" hello {name}"
        return value
```

## Creating Object

Creating an object of a class means making instances of the class.

```python
myobject = Myclass
```

 

## Accessing Methods and Attributes of a Class

Methods and attributes of a class can be accessed using the instance or object of the class.

Example, consider the mathematics class below.

```python
class Mathematics:

    pi = 3.14159
    num = 5

    def total( x, y ):
        return x + y

    def circle( radius ):
        return pi * pow( radius, 2)


#creating object

obj = Mathematics

#accessing attributes and methods

print( obj.num )                #output:  5
print( obj.total(4, 3)  )       #output:  7
print( obj.circle(8)  )         #output:  201.0618
```

 

## The init Method

The '__init__()' method is a class constructor used to initialize objects created from a class. It serves a role similar to the '*main()*' method in other programming languages like C, C++, and Dart. The '__init__()' method is where class attributes are declared, and the actual program execution or code processing begins.

The '__init__()' method takes at least one argument, which is typically named 'self'. The 'self' parameter refers to the instance of the class and is passed as the first parameter to the method. It allows class methods to access instance-specific attributes. Attributes declared within the '__init__()' method can be accessed and utilized by all functions or methods within the class that use the 'self' parameter.

Here's a basic example of using the '__init__()' method in a Python class:

```
</> Python

class Mathematics:

    def __init__( self ):
        self.pi = 3.14159
        self.num = 100

    def average( self, n ):
        avg =  self.num / n
        return avg

    def square( self ):
        return self.num ** 2


#creating object

obj = Mathematics

#accessing attributes and methods

print( obj.num )                #output:  100
print( obj.average(10)  )       #output:  10.0
print( obj.square()  )          #output:  9.869587728099999
```

 

# Handling Errors or Exceptions

Coding sometimes leads to various forms of errors, and it's essential to manage them when they occur. In programming, exception handling is a crucial concept for managing errors or unexpected issues that can arise during code execution. Errors in Python can be broadly categorized into two types: syntax errors and runtime errors.

## Syntax Error:

A syntax error occurs when the structure of a program does not adhere to the rules and syntax of the Python language. Common causes of syntax errors in Python include:

- Incorrect indentation.
- Missing colons.
- Empty blocks without the pass keyword.

## Runtime Error:

Runtime errors or exceptions occur during the execution of the program. These errors are not related to syntax but to issues that arise when code runs.

### Some runtime exceptions

| **Runtime error** | **Description** |
|---|---|
| ZeroDivisionError | A number is divided by zero |
| KeyError | A specific key is not found in a dictionary |
| NameError | A variable is not found in the local or global scope |
| IndexError | An index is out of range for a sequence |
| IndentationError | Wrong indentation in program |
| FloatingPointError | Operations on floating point fail |
| ImportError | Imported module is not found |
| AssertionError | Assertion statements fail |
| AttributeError | An invalid attribute reference or assignment is attempted |

 

| | |
|---|---|
| UnicodeError | An encoding or decoding operation fails |
| EOFError | The input() function reaches the end-of-file condition |

*Table 3.1: Some runtime errors in Python programming*

## Handling Exceptions

Python provides several mechanisms to catch and handle exceptions when they occur during program execution. Two fundamental constructs for exception handling are the try...except and try...finally statements.

### try...except

The code that may raise an exception is placed in the try block. If an exception occurs, the code in the except block is executed. ErrorType is optional and is used to handle specific types of errors.

Syntax

```python
try:
    #Code likely to raise an exception
except ErrorType:
    #Code to handle the exception
```

For example,

```python
try:
    var = 5
    result = var / 0        #zero division likely to raise exception
except ZeroDivisionError:
    print( "Error" )
```

 

## try...finally

In the try block, code likely to produce an error is placed. The finally block contains code that will be executed whether an exception is raised or not.

Syntax

```
</> Python

try:
    #Code likely to raise an exception
except ErrorType:
    #Code to handle the exception
finally:
    #Code that will be executed whether an exception is raised or not
```

For example,

```
</> Python
try:
    var = 5
    result = var / 0        #zero division likely to raise exception

except ZeroDivisionError:
    print( "Error" )

finally:
    print( "Awesome Python!" )
```

 

# Chapter Summary

### Variables and Identifiers

A variable, also known as an identifier, is a name assigned to store values in a computer's memory. Variables can contain letters, alphabets, or alphanumeric characters. However, Python reserves specific keywords that cannot be used as variable names because they serve predefined functions in the language.

Examples of Reserved Keywords in Python:

print, len, set, int, dict, list, object, import, exec, del, def, return, filter, min, complex, local, help, open, lambda

### Operators in Python

Operators are special symbols used in expressions to perform computations, comparisons, assignments, and logical operations. Python has several types of operators:

- Arithmetic Operators (e.g., +, -, *, /)
- Relational Operators (e.g., >, <, ==, !=)
- Assignment Operators (e.g., =, +=, -=)
- Logical Operators (e.g., and, or, not)
- Identity Operators (e.g., is, is not)
- Membership Operators (e.g., in, not in)
- Bitwise Operators (e.g., &, |, ^)

### Data Types in Python

Data types define the kind of values stored in variables. Python's fundamental data types include:

- Numbers (Integer and Float)
- String (Text data enclosed in quotes)
- List (Ordered, mutable collection)
- Dictionary (Key-value pairs)
- Tuple (Ordered, immutable collection)
- Set (Unordered, unique elements)
- Boolean (True or False)
- Bytes (Binary data representation)

# Chapter Summary

**Conditional Statements (Decision Making)**

Decision-making is essential in programming. Python uses if, elif, and else statements to execute code based on conditions. These statements evaluate Boolean values (True or False) and execute specific blocks accordingly.

**Loops (Repetitive Execution)**

Loops help execute a block of code multiple times. Python supports two primary loop structures:

- For loop – Iterates over a sequence (list, tuple, dictionary, etc.).
- While loop – Repeats execution as long as a condition remains true.

**Functions in Python**

A function is a reusable block of code designed to perform a specific task. Functions enhance code organization, reusability, and efficiency.

Importance of Functions

✓ Improved Readability – Functions break complex programs into logical sections, making the code easier to understand.
✓ Code Reusability – Avoids repetition by encapsulating repetitive tasks into functions.
✓ Modular Structure – Helps divide large programs into smaller, manageable parts.
✓ Time Efficiency – Speeds up development and debugging by structuring code logically.

## Keywords

| | | | |
|---|---|---|---|
| object-oriented | runtime | attribute | repetive |
| iterable | argument | mudularity | boolean |
| syntax | instance | procedures | intersection |

## Discussion

1. Functions help improve code efficiency and readability. Can you discuss a scenario where using functions would be beneficial in a real-world application?
2. What are some practical applications of Python's dictionary data structure? How does it compare to lists and tuples in terms of performance?
3. Why are membership and identity operators useful in Python? Can you provide examples of real-world use cases?
4. Error handling is an essential part of programming. How does Python handle errors using try-except blocks, and why is it important for writing robust programs?
5. How do arithmetic, relational, and logical operators work together in decision-making statements? Can you provide an example?
6. What are the advantages of using loops in a program? How does a for loop differ from a while loop in Python?

# Review Questions

1. Which of the following is a valid Python variable name?
   a) 1variable
   b) variable_1
   c) @var
   d) None

2. What will "hello".isidentifier() return?
   a) True
   b) False
   c) Error
   d) None

3. What is an **identifier** in Python?
   a) A reserved keyword
   b) A name used to identify variables, functions, etc.
   c) A type of function
   d) A built-in data type

4. Which of the following is **NOT** a valid identifier in Python?
   a) var_name
   b) _privateVar
   c) class
   d) myVar123

5. Which of these is a reserved keyword in Python?
   a) main
   b) def
   c) function
   d) define

6. What happens if you use a reserved keyword as a variable name?
   a) The program runs successfully
   b) The program crashes
   c) A syntax error occurs
   d) Python renames the variable automatically

7. Which of these is NOT a reserved keyword in Python?
   a) try
   b) finally
   c) end
   d) continue

8. What will 5 // 2 return?
   a) 2.5
   b) 2
   c) 3
   d) Error

9. Which of these is a logical operator in Python?
   a) &
   b) and
   c) +
   d) =

10. What does the membership operator in do?
    a) Checks if an item is present in a sequence
    b) Compares two numbers
    c) Performs bitwise operations
    d) Checks object identity

11. What is the type of 5.0 in Python?
    a) int
    b) float
    c) double
    d) long

12. Which of these is an immutable data type?
    a) list
    b) tuple
    c) dictionary
    d) set

13. Which data structure is best for storing key-value pa
    a) List
    b) Set
    c) Dictionary
    d) Tuple

14. What is the correct syntax for an if statement in Python?
    a) if x == 5 then:
    b) if (x == 5) {
    c) if x == 5:
    d) if x = 5:

15. Which of these is not a conditional statement?
    a) if
    b) while
    c) elif
    d) else

16. Which loop runs until a condition becomes false?
    a) for loop
    b) while loop
    c) do-while loop
    d) foreach loop

# Review Questions

What keyword is used to define a function in Python?
a) function
b) define
c) def
d) func

What will return do inside a function?
a) Stop the function execution and return a value
b) Print a value
c) Restart the function
d) Continue execution

What is an object in Python?
a) A built-in function
b) A class blueprint
c) An instance of a class
d) A reserved keyword

Which keyword is used to define a class in Python?
a) object
b) class
c) def
d) struct

What is self in Python classes?
a) A reference to the current instance
b) A special function
c) A reserved keyword
d) A built-in module

What keyword is used for exception handling in Python?
a) catch
b) handle
c) try
d) error

What happens if an error occurs in a try block but there's no except block?
a) The program crashes
b) Python fixes the error automatically
c) The error is ignored
d) The program continues execution

What is the output of print(type(5))?
a) float
b) int
c) str
d) bool

25. What does len([1, 2, 3]) return?
a) 1
b) 2
c) 3
d) None

26. What does the zip() function do in Python?
a) Compress files
b) Combine multiple lists into pairs
c) Sort a list
d) Join two strings

27. What is a variable in Python?
a) A reserved keyword
b) A name used to store a value
c) A function
d) A type of operator

28. Which of the following is NOT a valid data type in Python?
a) List
b) Tuple
c) Method
d) Dictionary

29. Which operator is used for logical comparisons in Python?
a) +
b) //
c) and
d) %

30. Which of the following is an immutable data type in Python?
a) List
b) Dictionary
c) Tuple
d) Set

31. What is the purpose of a function in Python?
a) To store a single value
b) To execute a block of code repeatedly
c) To perform a specific task and return a value
d) To define a new data type

32. Which Python statement is used to handle exceptions?
a) if-else
b) try-except
c) switch-case
d) do-while

Chapter

```
#Python
$pip install pillow
$pip install python-opencv
$pip install imageio

>>> from PIL import Image
>>> import cv2
>>> import imageio.v2
```

# PYTHON GRAPHICS

*After completing this chapter, you will be able to:*

- [x] Python modules
- [x] Python graphic modules

Ouereila Publishing House

# Python Graphics

Python is a powerful, ever-growing programming language with an extensive collection of libraries and modules. It is actively maintained by the Python Software Foundation and a large community of developers. Due to its simplicity, versatility, and efficiency, Python is widely used across numerous domains. It is not limited to just basic scripting; instead, it covers almost every technological field, including

- ☑ Science and Research
- ☑ Mathematics and Data Analysis
- ☑ Machine Learning and Artificial Intelligence
- ☑ Web Development
- ☑ Game Development
- ☑ Desktop and Mobile Application Development
- ☑ Cybersecurity and Ethical Hacking
- ☑ Networking and Automation
- ☑ Embedded Systems and IoT

Python has a vast ecosystem of libraries, some of which are specifically tailored for certain fields. These libraries simplify complex computations, automate tasks, and enhance functionality in various applications.

| **Domain** | **Modules** |
|---|---|
| Artificial Intelligence and Machine learning | TensorFlow, PyTorch, Scikit-learn, Keras, OpenCV |
| Web Development | Django, Flask, FastAPI, Tornado, Selenium, BeautifulSoup |
| Game Development | Pygame, Panda3D, Godot, Cocos2d, Arcade |
| Desktop and Mobile Apps (GUI Development) | PyQt, Flet, TKinter, Kivy/KivyMD, PySide, wxPython |
| Mathematics and Data Analysis | Numpy, SciPy, SymPy, Statsmodels |
| Cybersecurity and Ethical Hacking | Scapy, PyCrypto, Paramiko, Requests, Pwntools |
| Networking and Automation | Paramiko, Netmiko, PySNMP, Ansible, |
| Embedded Systems and IoT | MicroPython, CircuitPython, PySerial, RPi.GPIO |

*Table 4.0: Some Python libraries and their functional areas*

 

Python is not just for web or data science; it also plays a significant role in graphics and image processing. The language offers several libraries for app developers, data analysts, cybersecurity experts, game developers, website developers, and, most importantly, graphic designers. Python simplifies the implementation and design of graphics, including:

- Drawing shapes and patterns
- Animations and color conversions
- Image processing and editing
- Thresholding and segmentation
- Image detection and matching
- Face recognition
- Image and video analysis

Although there are several commercial and open-source graphic design software solutions such as Adobe Photoshop, GIMP, CorelDRAW, Inkscape, and Affinity Photo, Python allows you to achieve similar or even more powerful results through coding. The difference between using core Python for graphic design and commercial software like Adobe Photoshop is that Python allows you to programmatically design everything, controlling every aspect through code.

Python comes with built-in graphic modules, while others need to be installed via pip install. These modules range from basic drawing tools to complex AI-based image processing libraries.

## Python Graphics Libraries and Modules

The following table lists some of the most popular Python graphics-related libraries and their functionalities:

| Module | Installation | Functionality |
|---|---|---|
| Turtle | Pre-packaged | Simple geometric and pattern drawing |
| Pillow (PIL) | Pre-packaged | Image opening, manipulation (cropping, resizing, rotating, filtering) and format conversion |
| OpenCV | pip install opencv-python | Image processing, machine learning, AI-based image analysis |

 

| ImageIO | pip install imageio | Reading and writing images, videos and animations; format conversions |
|---|---|---|

*Table 4.1: Python Graphic libraries*

🚀 **Deep**

Did you know that you can create a complete graphic design software like Adobe Photoshop by integrating Python's logical capabilities with a graphical user interface (GUI)? Python provides several GUI frameworks and toolkits for mobile and desktop application development, allowing users to interact with graphical applications. Some of the most popular Python GUI frameworks include:

- 📌 PyQt or PySide (for advanced desktop applications)
- 📌 Tkinter (lightweight and built into Python)
- 📌 Flet (modern UI for cross-platform apps)
- 📌 Kivy/KivyMD (for mobile and touch-friendly applications)
- 📌 wxPython (for native-looking desktop applications)

With Python, you can build powerful and flexible graphics applications, from simple drawing tools to AI-powered image processing systems. This book focuses on using Python for graphic design and image processing, providing insights into various libraries and how to leverage them effectively.

 

# Chapter Summary

Python is a vast and ever-growing language with numerous libraries covering various fields, including science, mathematics, AI, web development, game development, and cybersecurity. It offers specialized modules for each domain, such as SciPy and Pandas for data analysis, NumPy for numerical computation, and TensorFlow for machine learning.

Python is also widely used for graphics and image processing. It enables tasks like drawing, animation image editing, face recognition, and video analysis. While commercial software like Adobe Photoshop and GIMP exist, Python allows developers to create similar tools programmatically.

Key Python graphics libraries include:

- Turtle (basic drawing)
- Pillow (image manipulation)
- OpenCV (image processing & AI)
- ImageIO (image/video handling)

For GUI-based applications, Python offers frameworks like PyQt, Tkinter, Flet, and Kivy, allowing developers to create interactive graphic design software.

## Key Terms

| | | | |
|---|---|---|---|
| versatility | UI | cropping | filtering |
| GUI | compilers | geometric | rotating |

## Discussion

1. How does Python's versatility make it suitable for various fields such as AI, web development, and game development?
2. What are the advantages of using Python for graphic design compared to commercial software like Adobe Photoshop and GIMP?
3. How does Python handle image processing through libraries like OpenCV and Pillow?
4. What are some real-world applications of Python in artificial intelligence and machine learning?
5. How do GUI frameworks like PyQt, Tkinter, and Kivy enhance the usability of Python-based graphic design applications?
6. What are the key differences between built-in Python modules and third-party libraries that require installation via pip?
7. How can Python be used for video processing and animation, and which libraries are best suited for this purpose?
8. What are the challenges of using Python for high-performance graphic design compared to traditional software tools?
9. How does the integration of AI and machine learning improve Python-based image processing?
10. What future advancements in Python libraries do you foresee in the fields of graphics and image processing?

# Review Questions

'hat makes Python a widely used programming uage?

is limited to web development
is difficult to learn
has numerous libraries covering various fields
does not support GUI applications

'hich of the following Python libraries is used for ntific computing and data analysis?

ensorFlow
andas
ask
ygame

'hich Python library is commonly used for hine learning and artificial intelligence?

:iPy
jango
ensorFlow
eautiful Soup

'hat is the primary function of the Pillow library thon?

'eb scraping
nage processing and manipulation
ame development
achine learning

hich GUI framework is built into Python and monly used for simple desktop applications?

Qt
kinter
vy
xPython

6. What is the main purpose of the OpenCV library?

A) Creating websites
B) Numerical computation
C) Image processing and computer vision
D) Data analysis

7. Which of the following Python libraries is primarily used for game development?

A) PyTorch
B) Selenium
C) Pygame
D) Scapy

8. Which command is used to install third-party Python packages like OpenCV?

A) install OpenCV
B) python install OpenCV
C) pip install opencv-python
D) setup install opencv-python

9. What is the role of Flet and Kivy in Python development?

A) Database management
B) Machine learning
C) Frontend GUI development
D) Web scraping

10. Which Python module is pre-packaged and used for simple geometric and pattern drawing?

A) SimpleCV
B) Turtle
C) Seaborn
D) NumPy

```
#Python

$pip install pillow

>>> import PIL
>>> img=Image.open()
>>> img.height
>>> img.size
>>>ImageDraw.Draw()
```

# Pillow (PIL)

*After completing this chapter, you will be able to:*

- ☑ Understand the features and functionalities of Python Pillow
- ☑ Understand the various file formats
- ☑ Utilize the PIL image modules effectively
- ☑ Explore the Image module for image manipulation
- ☑ Use the ImageDraw module for drawing on images
- ☑ Enhances image using the ImageEnhance module
- ☑ Apply effects and transformations with the ImageFilter module
- ☑ Perform advance image operations using the ImageChops module
- ☑ Capture screenshots with the ImageGrab module

# Pillow (PIL)

Pillow, also known as **PIL (Python Imaging Library),** is a core Python module for loading, manipulating, enhancing, and processing images in various formats. It provides a wide range of image-processing capabilities that allow developers to modify images programmatically. Pillow enables tasks such as image resizing, cropping, rotating, filtering, and format conversion, making it an essential tool for applications that involve image processing.

## Features and Functionalities

### ✎ Loading, Showing, and Printing Images
Pillow allows users to load images from different file formats and display them directly. Additionally, it provides the capability to print image details such as size, mode, and format.

### ✎ Creating Images from Scratch
Developers can generate images from scratch using Pillow, defining colors, sizes, and shapes as needed. This feature is particularly useful for creating placeholders, patterns, or visual data representations.

### ✎ Image Rotation
Pillow provides built-in methods to rotate images at various angles. This feature is useful in applications requiring image orientation adjustments, such as correcting tilted photos.

### ✎ Image Cropping
Images can be cropped to extract specific areas of interest. This feature is commonly used in applications requiring face detection, object recognition, or automated document processing.

### ✎ Scaling Images
Resizing images while maintaining aspect ratio is an essential function in many applications. Pillow enables users to scale images to fit different screen sizes or optimize them for various platforms.

 

### ✏️ Image Filtering

Pillow provides filtering capabilities to enhance images, including sharpening, blurring, and edge detection. These features improve image quality and can be used for artistic effects or pre-processing in machine learning applications.

### ✏️ Image File Format Conversion

Pillow supports converting images from one file format to another. This functionality is useful for optimizing images for different use cases, such as converting a high-resolution PNG to a more storage-efficient JPEG.

### ✏️ Color Transformation

The library allows changing an image's color mode, such as converting an image from RGB to grayscale. This is useful for reducing file size, improving contrast, or preparing images for further analysis.

### ✏️ Resizing Images

Pillow provides methods to resize images while preserving quality. This feature is particularly useful for creating thumbnails or optimizing images for web applications.

### ✏️ Retrieving Image Statistics

The library includes a histogram method that allows users to analyze pixel distribution within an image. This feature is commonly used in image recognition, segmentation, and color analysis applications.

## Installation and Compatibility

While Pillow is often pre-installed with Python, some environments may require manual installation. It is important to ensure that PIL is not installed alongside Pillow, as they may not coexist properly.

> **📝 Note**
>
> In case of compatibility issues, it is recommended to uninstall PIL before installing Pillow.
>
> 📌 pip uninstall PIL
> 📌 pip install pillow

Pillow remains a powerful and versatile tool for image processing in Python, supporting a wide range of functionalities suitable for beginners and advanced users alike. Whether for simple tasks such as resizing and cropping or complex operations like filtering and transformation, Pillow provides a robust solution for handling images programmatically.

## Image File Formats

Pillow (PIL) is a powerful image processing library capable of handling various image file formats across different operating systems. It allows seamless conversion between formats while preserving image quality. An image can be loaded in one format, processed, and saved in another without loss of essential details.

### Supported Image Formats and Platforms

Pillow supports a wide range of image file formats commonly used across multiple platforms:

| Format | Extension(s) | Description | Platforms |
|---|---|---|---|
| JPEG / JFIF | .jpg, .jpeg | Common image format, lossy compression | Windows, macOS, Linux |
| JPEG 2000 | .jp2, .j2k, .jpx | Advanced JPEG format with better compression | Windows, macOS, Linux |
| PNG | .png | Portable Network Graphics, supports transparency | Windows, macOS, Linux |
| TIFF | .tif, .tiff | Tagged Image File Format, used in professional photography | Windows, macOS, Linux |
| ICO | .ico | Windows icon format | Windows |
| ICNS | .icns | macOS icon format | macOS |
| GIF | .gif | Graphics Interchange Format, supports animation | Windows, macOS, Linux |
| PPM/PGM/PBM | .ppm, .pgm, .pbm | Portable Pixmap/Graymap/Bitmap | Unix-based systems |
| SGI | .sgi, .rgb, .rgba, .bw | Silicon Graphics Image format | Windows, macOS, Linux |
| MSP | .msp | Microsoft Paint format (old versions) | Windows |
| PCX | .pcx | Paintbrush image format | Windows |
| BMP | .bmp | Bitmap image format | Windows, macOS, Linux |
| DDS | .dds | DirectDraw Surface, used in game textures | Windows, macOS, Linux |
| DIB | .dib | Device-independent bitmap | Windows |
| EPS | .eps | Encapsulated PostScript | Windows, macOS, Linux |
| IM | .im | A format used by LabEye and other applications | Windows, macOS, Linux |

 

| WEBP | .webp | Modern web image format with better compression | Windows, macOS, Linux |
|---|---|---|---|
| TGA | .tga | Truevision TGA, used in 3D graphics and gaming | Windows, macOS, Linux |
| XPM | .xpm | X PixMap, used in X11 applications | Unix-based systems |
| XBM | .xbm | X Bitmap, used in X11 GUI systems | Unix-based systems |
| SPIDER | .spi | Multi-image format used in electron microscopy | Windows, macOS, Linux |
| PFM | .pfm | Portable Float Map, used in high-precision images | Windows, macOS, Linux |
| FITS | .fli, .flc | Flexible Image Transport System, used in astronomy | Windows, macOS, Linux |
| CUR | .cur | Windows cursor format | Windows |
| MIC | .mic | Microsoft Image Composer format | Windows |
| PSD | .psd | Adobe Photoshop format | Windows, macOS, Linux |
| WMF, EMF | .wmf, .emf | Windows Metafile / Enhanced Metafile, used for vector graphics | Windows |

*Table 5.0: Supported Image File Formats in Pillow*

**Deep**

With Pillow's image file conversion capabilities, you can easily convert an image from one format to another, including converting images to PDF.

## The PIL Modules

Pillow (PIL) consists of several modules, each designed to provide specialized classes and methods for handling different aspects of image processing. These modules focus on various functionalities such as image filtering, color manipulation, special effects, image composition, painting, 2D graphics, and other advanced graphic features. Each class within these modules offers distinct methods that enable efficient image and graphic processing.

 

## Some essential Pillow modules

✅ **Image Module (PIL.Image)**

- Provides the core functionality for opening, creating, and saving images.
- Supports multiple image formats.

✅ **ImageChops Module (PIL.ImageChops)**

- Supports image arithmetic and logical operations.
- Used for blending, compositing, and enhancing images.

✅ **ImageEnhance Module (PIL.ImageEnhance)**

- Provides methods to adjust brightness, contrast, sharpness, and color balance.

✅ **ImageFilter Module (PIL.ImageFilter)**

- Offers predefined filters such as BLUR, CONTOUR, DETAIL, EDGE_ENHANCE, SHARPEN, etc.

✅ **ImageDraw Module (PIL.ImageDraw)**

- Allows drawing shapes, lines, and text onto images.

✅ **ImageFont Module (PIL.ImageFont)**

- Handles different font styles for rendering text on images.

✅ **ImageGrab Module (PIL.ImageGrab)**

- Captures screenshots (Windows and macOS only).

### Note

Pillow includes many modules, some of which extend beyond the scope of this book. The modules listed above are essential for graphic design.

### Deep

There are four simple ways to utilize the modules or classes provided by PIL:

1. Importing a single module by its name from PIL.
   ```
   >>> from PIL import Image
   ```

2. Importing multiple modules from PIL at once.
   ```
   >>> from PIL import Image, ImageDraw, ImageFilter
   ```

 

3. Importing all classes using the * wildcard.
```
>>> from PIL import *
```

4. Importing PIL and creating instances of classes when needed.
```
>>> import PIL
>>> img = PIL.Image.open('mypicture.jpg')
```

## The Image Module

The **Image** module in Pillow provides a class with various methods, each offering unique functionalities for handling images. This module allows you to open, load, display, rotate, create, crop, and retrieve image information seamlessly.

**Methods** — Pillow (PIL)

| | | | |
|---|---|---|---|
| open | show | blend | core |
| close | save | alpha_composite | deprecate |
| new | merge | annotation | effect_noise |
| frombyte | split | atexit | enum |
| frombuffer | math | builtins | eval |
| module | abc | cast | fromarray |
| fromqimage | fromqpixmap | getmodebans | getmodebase |
| getmodetype | init | io | is_path |
| item | linear_gradient | logger | logging |
| preinit | os | radia_gradient | re |
| isImageType | register_extensions | register_save | register_open |
| tempfile | register_mime | register_save_all | registered_extensions |

 

### show( )

Displays the image using the system's default image viewer. It creates a temporary file to preview the image.

### new( mode, size, color )

The new() method creates a new image from scratch by specifying its mode, size, and color.
mode →(string): Defines the type of color bands (e.g., "RGB", "RGBA", "L", or "CMYK").
size → (float,float): A 2-tuple (width, height) representing the image dimensions.
color → *(Optional)*: Defines the image color as:

- A single integer (e.g., 156).
- An RGB or RGBA tuple (red, green, blue, alpha).
- A string representing a color name (e.g., "red").
- A hex color name (e.g., "# F5F8FA").

</> Python

```
from PIL import  Image
img =  Image.new( mode = "RGBA", size = (600, 800), color = "#1DA1F2")
img.show( )
```

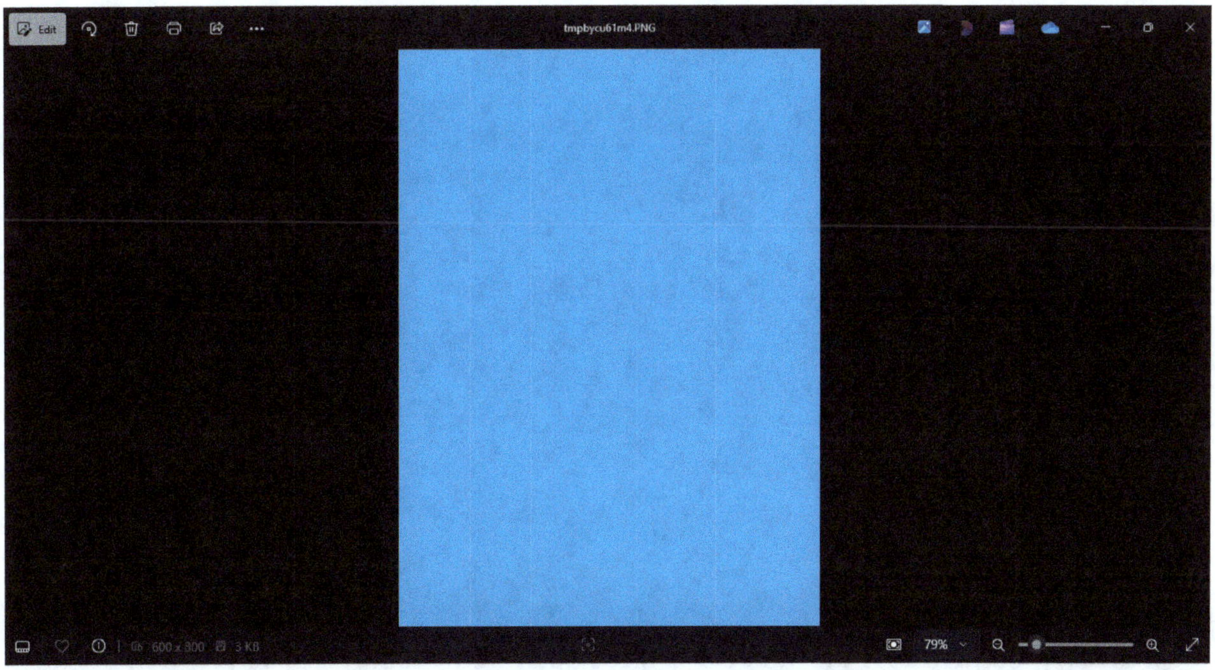


 

open( path, mode, format )

This method loads an image from a specified path.

path → (string): The file location (as a string or bytes).

mode → (string) [Optional]: Specifies read 'r' (default) or write 'w'.

format → (Optional): Defines the format if not inferred from the file.

Methods and Attributes of an Open Image

| height | custom_mimetype | format | getexif | save |
|---|---|---|---|---|
| app | decoderconfig | fp | getextrema | seek |
| applist | decodermaxblock | frombytes | getim | show |
| histogram | get_format_mimetype | entropy | getpalette | size |
| bits | effect_spread | filename | getpixel | split |
| close | get_child_images | getbands | getprojection | tell |
| convert | has_transparency_data | getchannel | getxmp | thumbnail |
| copy | apply_transparency | getcolors | load_djpeg | tile |
| crop | alpha_composite | getdata | load_prepare | tobitmap |
| draft | format_description | filter | quantization | transform |
| icclist | putpalette | load_read | quantize | transpose |
| info | putpixel | point | readonly | verify |
| layer | palette | putalpha | reduce | width |
| mode | paste | putdata | remap_palette | resize |
| rotate | | | | |

*Table 5.1: Some Available Methods of an Open Image*

## Deep

To retrieve the methods and attributes of an image opened with **Image.open()**, use the **dir()** function on the image object.

```
>>> img  = Image.open("path/to/image.jpg")
>>> dir(img)
```

## Think about it ?

The **close()** method closes the image and frees up system resources, such as memory and file handles, that were allocated when the image was opened for editing. What other specific resources does it release?

 

```python
from PIL import Image
img = Image.open("flower_girl.jpg")
img.show( )
```

## Saving Images and File Conversion

save( fp, format, save_all, append_images, loop, duration, quality, disposal, transparency, interlace )

The save() method in Pillow plays a crucial role in saving and converting images. It provides multiple functionalities depending on the file format used. For instance, saving an image as a GIF requires parameters that might not be applicable when saving as a JPEG.

### Key Functions of save()

- ✏️ Saving an edited or manipulated image as a new file.
- ✏️ Converting an image from one format to another.
- ✏️ Stacking multiple images into a single file.
- ✏️ Creating animated images such as GIFs.

#### Parameters

fp →(str) [required]: The filename or file path to save the image. The file extension must be included (e.g., "myimage.jpg").

format →(str) [Optional]: Specifies the file format (e.g., "JPEG", "PNG", "GIF"). If omitted, the format is inferred from fp.

save_all →(bool) [Optional]: If True, saves all frames of a multi-frame image (e.g., GIF). Default is False, which saves only the first frame.

append_images →(list of Image objects) [Optional]: A list of additional images to be appended, useful for stacking images or creating animations.

loop →(int) [Optional, GIF-specific]: Specifies how many times an animated image should loop. 0 means infinite looping.

duration →(int) [Optional, GIF-specific]: Sets the display duration (in milliseconds) for each frame in an animated image.

quality →(int) [Optional, JPEG-specific]: Determines the quality of the saved image (1 to 95). Higher values yield better quality. Default is 75.

disposal →(int)[Optional, GIF-specific]: Determines how the previous frame is handled in animations. Default is 0.

transparency →(int or None)[Optional, GIF/PNG-specific]: Defines a transparency color index.

 

interlace →(bool)[Optional, PNG-specific]: If True, enables interlacing for progressive loading.

</> Python

```
from PIL import  Image
img =  Image.open("flower_girl.jpg")
img.save( "new_image.jpg" )
```

Deep

You can convert an image to a different format by changing the file extension in the filename.

```
>>> from PIL import  Image
>>> img =  Image.open("image.jpg")
>>> img.save( "myimage.png" )          # conversion from JPG to PNG
```

## Creating GIFs or Animated Images

</> Python

```
from PIL import  Image
img1 = Image.open("image1.jpg").resize(size=(600, 800))
img2 = Image.open("image2.jpg").resize(size=(600, 800))
img3 = Image.open("image3.jpg").resize(size=(600, 800))

imgs = [ img2, img3]

img1.save(fp="animate.gif", save_all= True, append_images= imgs, duration= 5, loop=0)
```

 

## Creating PDFs

</> Python

```python
from PIL import  Image
pic1 = Image.open("picture1.jpg").resize(size=(600, 800))
pic2 = Image.open("picture2.jpg").resize(size=(600, 800))
pic3 = Image.open("picture3.jpg").resize(size=(600, 800))

imgs = [ pic2, pic3]

pic1.save(fp="sample.pdf", format="PDF", save_all= True, append_images= imgs)
```

**Think about it ?**

A multi-frame image is a single file that contains multiple images, allowing for animation or layered content. Formats that support multi-frame images include **GIF** and **TIFF**, which can store multiple frames within one file. What other formats support multi-frame images?

## Color Conversion and Filters

Pillow provides various methods for converting colors, applying filters, and manipulating image color channels. These functions help in changing image modes, adjusting transparency, and processing pixel values.

 

### convert( mode, colors )

The **convert()** method is used to change an image from one color mode to another.

mode →(string)[optional] : Specifies the target color mode. Common modes include:

- RGB - Red, Green, Blue
- CMYK - Cyan, Magenta, Yellow, Black
- L - Luminance (grayscale)
- RGBA - RGB with an Alpha (transparency) channel
- LAB, HSV, P, 1, I, F - Other modes for various image types

colors →(optional): An integer (0–256) specifying the number of colors when using the Palette.ADAPTIVE mode.

```python
from PIL import Image
img = Image.open("flower_girl.jpg")

gray_image = img.convert( mode = "L" )
img.show( )                 # showing the original image
gray_image.show( )          # showing a gray image
```

**Note**

In grayscale conversion, the formula used is:
L=(R×299/1000)+(G×587/1000)+(B×114/1000)L = (R \times 299/1000) + (G \times 587/1000) + (B \times 114/1000)L=(R×299/1000)+(G×587/1000)+(B×114/1000)
Where: R = Red, G = Green, B = Blue

### putalpha( alpha )

This method adjusts the transparency (alpha) of an image.

alpha →(int): An integer that defines the transparency level. Lower values increase transparency. A value of **1** makes the image almost completely invisible.

**Python**

```
from PIL import Image
img = Image.open("flower_girl.jpg")
copied = img.copy( )          # creates a copy of the image
img.putalpha( alpha = 100 )
copied.putalpha( alpha = 20 )
img.show( )                   # showing first image with alpha 100
copied.show( )                # showing second image with alpha 20
```

point( lut )

It applies a function to modify pixel values across all bands in the image.

lut →(function): A required function that takes a single argument and returns a new pixel value.

</> Python

```python
from PIL import  Image

img =  Image.open("africa.jpg")
inverted = img.point( lut = lambda x: 255 - x )   # this function inverts each pixel's value

img.show( )            # showing the original image
inverted.show( )       # showing an inverted image (dark areas become white and white area, dark)
```

## split( ) and merge(mode, bands)

The *splits()* divides an image into individual color bands. This is useful for processing specific channels separately. For example,
Splitting an RGB image results in three separate images for Red, Green, and Blue.

The *merge()* combines individual image bands into a single image.
mode : The target mode for merging, such as "RGB" or "CMYK".
bands : A sequence of images, each representing a single color channel.

</> Python

```python
from PIL import Image

img = Image.open("africa.jpg")
r, g, b = img.split( )          # splitting image into 3 color bands ( red, green, blue)
r.show( )
g.show( )
b.show( )

merged_img = Image.merge( mode= "RGB" , bands = [ r, g, b] )     # merging the color bands
merged_img.show( )
```

Red color band

Green color band

*Blue color band*

*Merged color bands ( bands = [ r, g, b])*

*Merged color bands (bands = [ b, g, r])*

*Merged color bands ( bands = [ g, b, r])*

**Think about it ?**

1. Why do the images above show only slight differences in their color bands?
2. Why do the images appear in grayscale even in the red, green, and blue color bands?
3. Can you identify the subtle differences between them?

 

## Geometric Transformations

Image Transformation refers to modifying an image's structure, size, orientation, or content without altering its core data. Pillow provides various transformation methods such as resizing, rotating, cropping, and pasting images. These transformations allow precise control over how images appear and are processed.

resize(size, box, resample)

The resize() method is used to scale an image up or down, modifying its width and height.
size → (width, height): A required 2-tuple defining the new dimensions.
box → (left, top, right, bottom): An optional 4-tuple specifying the region to be scaled.
resample: Defines the resampling filter (e.g., Image.Resampling.NEAREST, Image.Resampling.BILINEAR, Image.Resampling.BICUBIC).

</> Python

```
from PIL import Image

img = Image.open("bird.jpg")
resized = img.resize(size= (600, 800 ) )
resized_with_box = img.resize(size= (600, 800 ), box =(0, 0, 400, 600 ) )

resized.show( )
resized_with_box.show( )
```

reduce(factor, box)

The reduce() method scales down an image by a given factor while preserving quality.
factor →(int or 2-tuple) : Required parameter defining the reduction ratio.
box → (left, top, right, bottom): Optional 4-tuple specifying a region to be reduced.

</> Python

```
from PIL import  Image

img =  Image.open("bird.jpg")
reduced = img.reduce( factor= 5 )
img.show( )
reduced.show( )
```

**Deep**

The thumbnail( size, resample) method resizes an image to fit within a bounding box while maintaining its aspect ratio.

- size: *(width, height)* — A 2-tuple defining the maximum size.
- resample: Defines the resampling filter (same as resize).

 

rotate( angle, center, fillcolor, resample, expand, translate)

The **rotate()** method rotates an image by a given angle around a specified center point.

angle → (float): Rotation angle in degrees.

center → (x, y): Optional 2-tuple defining the pivot point.

fillcolor → (int or tuple): Optional color for the empty areas.

expand → (bool): If True, resizes the output to fit the entire rotated image.

translate → (x, y): Optional 2-tuple shifting the image.

resample: Defines the resampling filter (same as resize). The available filters include,

| | | |
|---|---|---|
| Resampling.NEAREST | Resampling.BILINEAR | Resampling.BICUBIC |
| Resampling.BOX | Resampling.HAMMING | Resampling.LANCZOS |

```
</> Python
img =  Image.open("bird.jpg")

rotation_180 = img.rotate( angle=180)
rotation_90=img.rotate( angle=90, expand=True, resample=Image.Resampling.BICUBIC)
rotation_45 = img.rotate( angle= 45, expand= True, fillcolor="red")
rotation_135 = img.rotate( angle= 135, expand= True, center= (300,300))

rotation_180.show()
rotation_90.show()
rotation_45.show()
rotation_135.show()
```

180° rotation

90° rotation

45° rotation

135° rotation

**Note**

Image.Resampling.BOX is not supported for rotation.

## transpose(method)

The transpose() method provides predefined rotation and flipping options: The available defined rotation methods are,

| Methods | Description |
|---|---|
| Image.Transpose.ROTATE_90 | Rotates 90° counterclockwise. |
| Image.Transpose.ROTATE_180 | Rotates 180°. |
| Image.Transpose.ROTATE_270 | Rotates 270°. |
| Image.Transpose.FLIP_LEFT_RIGHT | Flips the image horizontally. |
| Image.Transpose.FLIP_TOP_BOTTOM | Flips the image vertically. |
| Image.Transpose.TRANSVERSE | Rotating 90° counterclockwise, then flipping horizontally |
| Image.Transpose.TRANSPOSE | Rotating 90° clockwise, then flipping vertically. |

*Table 5.2 : Defined rotation methods*

 

```python
from PIL import Image
img = Image.open(“bird.jpg”)

transpose = img.transpose( Image.Transpose.TRANSPOSE)
transverse = img.transpose( Image.Transpose.TRANSVERSE)
transpose_90 = img.transpose( Image.Transpose.ROTATE_90)
transpose_180 = img.transpose( Image.Transpose.ROTATE_180)
transpose.show()
transverse.show()
transpose_90.show()
transpose_180.show()
```

TRANSPOSE

TRANSVERSE

ROTATE_90

ROTATE_180

 

### crop(box) and paste(image, box, mask)

The **crop()** extracts a rectangular region from an image.
box →(left, top, right, bottom): A 4-tuple defining the region to extract.

The **paste()** pastes or places an image onto another image at a specified position.
image: The source image to paste.
box → (left, top): Optional coordinates for positioning.
mask →(Image or None): An optional mask for transparency.

</> Python

```python
from PIL import  Image
puppy1 = Image.open("puppy1.jpg")
puppy2 = Image.open("puppy2.jpg")

puppy1.show()
puppy2.show()

cropped = puppy1.crop(box= (200, 200, 600,1000) )   # extracting a region from puppy1
puppy2.paste(im= cropped, box = (10, 500) )
puppy2.show()
```

*Puppy1*

*Puppy2*

*puppy1 pasted into puppy2*

## Image Attributes

Pillow provides several attributes for retrieving essential information about an image. These attributes help in understanding the image's format, size, color composition, and more.

 

### filename and format

The *filename* returns the full name of the image file, including its extension.
The *format* returns the image file format, such as "JPEG", "PNG", or "GIF". This corresponds to the file extension of the image.

```
</> Python
>>> from PIL import Image
>>> img = Image.open("flower_girl.jpg")
>>> img.filename
'flower_girl.jpg'
>>> img.format
'JPEG'
>>>
```

### width, height and size

The *width* returns the width of the image in pixel.
The *height* method returns the height of the image in pixel.
The size() returns the width and height of the image as a tuple (width, height).

```
</> Python
>>> from PIL import Image
>>> img = Image.open("flower_girl.jpg")
>>> img.width
736
>>> img.height
920
>>> img.size
(736, 920)          # (width, height)
>>>
```

### getpixel( xy ) and histogram(maxcolors)

The *getpixel()* returns the pixel value at a specific (x, y) coordinate. The returned value format depends on the image mode.

The *histogram*() method returns a histogram of the image, representing pixel intensity distribution. This is useful for analyzing image contrast and color composition.

 

```
</> Python
>>> from PIL import Image
>>> img =  Image.open("flower_girl.jpg")
>>> img.getpixel( xy = (10, 20))
(190, 190, 182)
>>> img.histogram()
[.........]                    # List of pixels
>>>
```

### mode, getbands() and getcolors()

The *mode* returns the color mode of the image, defining the number and type of color bands. Common modes include:

- **RGB** – Red, Green, Blue
- **CMYK** – Cyan, Magenta, Yellow, Black
- **L** – Luminance (grayscale)
- **RGBA** – RGB with an Alpha (transparency) channel
- **LAB**, **HSV**, **P**, **1**, **I**, **F** – Other modes for various image types

The *getbands()* returns a tuple listing the names of each color band in the image. For an **RGB** image, it returns ('R', 'G', 'B').

The *getcolors()* returns a list of colors used in the image, limited to the specified maxcolors (default: 256). Returns None if the color count exceeds the limit.

```
</> Python
>>> from PIL import Image
>>> img =  Image.open("pictures\\cat.jpg")
>>> img.mode
'RGB'
>>> img.getbands()
('R', 'G', 'B')
>>>
```

 

# The ImageDraw Module

The **ImageDraw** module in the Python Imaging Library (PIL) provides methods for drawing 2D graphics, including shapes, geometric figures, and text, onto images. It is used alongside the Image module to create and manipulate images.

**Methods** — Pillow (PIL)

| Any | Draw | ModuleType | annotations |
|---|---|---|---|
| AnyStr | Image | Outline | cast |
| Callable | ImageColor | Sequence | deprecate |
| Coords | ImageDraw | Union | floodfill |
| getdraw | math | struct | |

**Deep**

Use dir(ImageDraw) to list all the methods and attributes available in the **ImageDraw** module.

```
>>> from PIL import ImageDraw, Image
>>> dir(ImageDraw)
[.........]
>>>
>>> img = Image.open("picture.ico")
>>> draw = ImageDraw.Draw(im = img)
>>> dir(draw)
[.........]
>>>
```

 

### Draw( im, mode )

The **Draw()** class is crucial for adding graphics to images. It provides numerous functions for drawing geometric shapes and applying text.
im →(Image)[required]: A required parameter that specifies the image to be drawn on.
mode → (string)[optional]: Specifies the color mode, such as "RGB", "L", or "CMYK".

Methods and Attributes of Draw

| arc | ellipse | im | multiline_textbbox | rectangle |
|---|---|---|---|---|
| bitmap | fill | ink | palette | regular_polygon |
| chord | font | line | pieslice | rounded_rectangle |
| circle | fontmode | mode | point | shape |
| draw | getfont | multiline_text | polygon | text |
| textbbox | textlength | | | |

*Table 5.3: Some methods of Draw()*

### text( xy, text, fill, font, fill, spacing, align, direction, stroke_width, stroke_fill, embedded_color )

The **text()** method is used to add text to an image.
xy →(tuple (x, y)): Specifies the coordinates where the text should appear.
text →(string): The actual text to be displayed.
font →(ImageFont) [optional]: Defines the font style. Example: ImageFont.truetype("path/to/font.ttf", size).
fill → (int/str/tuple) [optional]: Defines the text color.
spacing →(float) [optional]: Sets the space between lines in multiline text.
align → (string) = ("left", "right", "center"): Controls text alignment.
direction → (string) = ("ltr", "rtl", "ttb"): Specifies text direction.
stroke_width →(float) [optional]: Sets the stroke thickness.
stroke_fill →(color) [optional]: Defines the stroke color.
embedded_color →(bool)[optional]: Determines whether to use font-embedded color glyphs.

 

Python

```python
from PIL import Image, ImageDraw, ImageFont

img  = Image.new(mode="RGB", size=(600,800), color="#324D34")
draw = ImageDraw.Draw(im=img)

font = ImageFont.load_default(size=50)
mytext = "Awesome Python!\nGraphics"
draw.text(text=mytext, xy=(100, 350), font=font, align= "center" )
img.show()
```

Deep

The **ImageFont** module in PIL is used for customizing fonts.

The **ImageFont.load_default(size)** method adjusts the default font size. To use a custom font, **ImageFont.truetype(font, size, index)** is used, where **font** specifies the font file, **size** defines the font size, and **index** indicates the font face to load.

```
>>> from PIL import ImageFont
>>> font = ImageFont.truetype( font= "san_serif.ttf", size = 20)
>>>
```

You can explore and download fonts from Google Fonts.

 

```python
from PIL import Image, ImageDraw, ImageFont

smile  = Image.open("smile.jpg")
draw = ImageDraw.Draw(im=smile)
font = ImageFont.truetype(font="font.ttf", size=50)
text = "smile with love"
draw.text(text=text, xy=(50, smile.height-200), font=font, align= "center", fill="#D86350" )

eagle  = Image.open("eagle.jpeg")
draw = ImageDraw.Draw(im=eagle)
font = ImageFont.truetype(font="arvo.ttf", size=60)
text = "The power of courage!"
draw.text(text=text, xy=(20, 500), font=font, align= "center", stroke_fill="#ff6700", stroke_width=50)

smile.show()
eagle.show()
```

**Deep**

Multiline Text

The **multiline_text()** method has the same parameters as text(), but it is specifically designed to render text containing newline characters (\n).

## Drawing Shapes

line(xy, fill, width, joint)

The **line()** method draws a line by connecting coordinate points.

xy →(list of (x, y) tuples): Points defining the line path.

width →(float) [optional]: Line thickness.

fill →(color)[optional]: Line color.

</> **Python**

```python
from PIL import Image, ImageDraw

line  = Image.new(mode="RGB", size=(800, 600), color="#3a6ea5")
draw = ImageDraw.Draw(im=line)
draw.line(xy= [(100,300), (400, 200), (450, 400), (750, 300)], width= 5, fill="#ebebeb")
line.show()
```

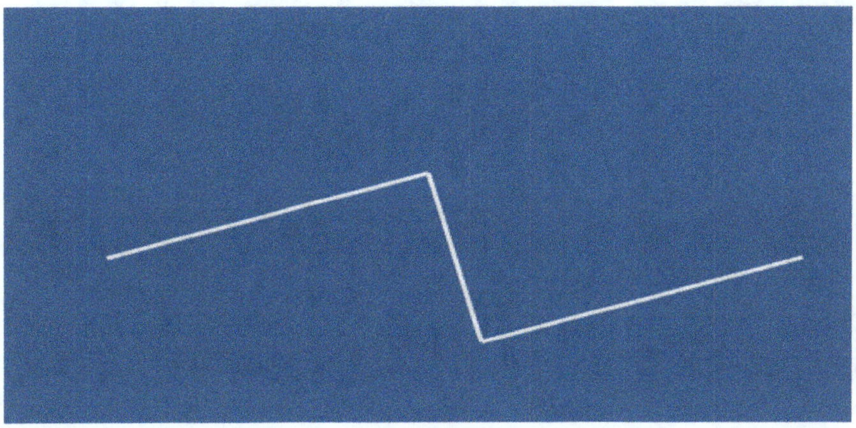

 

rectangle(xy, fill, outline, width)

The **rectangle()** method is used to draw a rectangular shape on an image.

xy →(tuple or list of tuples (x, y, width, height)): Defines the rectangle coordinates.

fill →(color)[optional]: Background color.

outline →(color) [optional]: Border color.

width →(float)[optional]: Border thickness.

**Note**

The **rectangle()** method can also be used to draw squares. This can be achieved by ensuring that the coordinates define equal side lengths.

</> **Python**

```
from PIL import Image, ImageDraw

rectangle  = Image.new(mode="RGB", size=(500,500), color="#3a6ea5")
draw_rec = ImageDraw.Draw(im=rectangle)
draw_rec.rectangle(xy= (100,100, 400, 300), width= 2, fill="#ebebeb")

square  = Image.new(mode="RGB", size=(500,500), color="#3a6ea5")
draw_sq = ImageDraw.Draw(im=square)
draw_sq.rectangle(xy= (100,100, 400,400), width= 5, outline="#ebebeb")

rectangle.show()
square.show()
```

*rectangle*

*square*

 

rounded_rectangle(xy, fill, outline, width)

The **rounded_rectangle()** method is used to draw a rectangle with rounded corners.

radius →(float): Defines corner rounding.

xy →(tuple or list of tuples (x, y, width, height)): Defines the rectangle coordinates.

fill →(color)[optional]: Background color.

outline →(color)[optional]: Border color.

width →(float)[optional]: Border thickness.

</> Python

```python
from PIL import Image, ImageDraw
round_rec  = Image.new(mode="RGB", size=(500,500), color="#324D34")
draw = ImageDraw.Draw(im=round_rec)
draw.rounded_rectangle(radius= 25, xy= (100,150, 400, 300), width= 2, fill="#ebebeb")

round_rec_pic  = Image.open("girl.jpeg")
draw2 = ImageDraw.Draw(im=round_rec_pic)
xy = (100,100, round_rec_pic.width-100, round_rec_pic.height-100)
draw2.rounded_rectangle( radius= 20, xy= xy, width= 5, outline="#c57284")
round_rec.show()
round_rec_pic.show()
```

 | 

circle(xy, radius, outline, width, fill)

The **circle()** method is used to draw a circle with a defined radius and center point.

xy →(x, y) [required]: Defines the center coordinates of the circle.

radius →(float) [required]: Specifies the radius of the circle.

width → (float)[required]: Determines the thickness of the circle's outline.

outline → (int or "string" or "#hex" or (red, green, blue))[optional]: Specifies the boundary color of the circle.

fill → (int or "string", "#hex" or (red, green, blue))[optional]: Defines the background color of the circle. It is transparent by default.

</> Python

```python
from PIL import Image, ImageDraw

circle  = Image.new(mode="RGB", size=(500,500), color="#151419")
draw = ImageDraw.Draw(im=circle)
draw.circle(radius= 100, xy = (250,250,), width= 5, fill="#EB5E28")

circle_pic  = Image.open("potrait.jpg")
draw2 = ImageDraw.Draw(im = circle_pic)
draw2.circle( radius= 200, xy =  (370,300) , width= 10, outline="#EB5E28")

circle.show()
circle_pic.show()
```

ellipse(xy, width, outline, fill)

The **ellipse()** is used to draw circles by specifying a bounding box.

xy → (x, y, width, height) [required]: Defines the center coordinates of the circle.

width → (float)[optional]: Determines the thickness of the circle's outline.

outline → (int, "string", "#hex" or (red, green, blue)) [optional]: Specifies the boundary color of the circle.

fill → (int, "string", "#hex" or (red, green, blue)) [optional]: Defines the background color of the ellipse. It is transparent by default.

</> Python

```python
from PIL import Image, ImageDraw

img  = Image.new(mode="RGB", size=(500,500), color="#3A6EA5")
draw = ImageDraw.Draw(im=img)
draw.ellipse(xy= (100, 100, 400, 400), width= 20, outline="#0D2137", fill="#ebebeb")
draw.ellipse(xy= (150, 150, 350, 350), width= 10, fill="red")
img.show()
```

arc(xy, start, end, width, fill)

The **arc()** method draws an incomplete circle or a portion of a circle outline..

xy → (x, y, width, height) [required]: Defines the center coordinates of the circle.

start , end → (float) [required]: Define the start and end angles of the arc.

width → (float) [optional]: Determines the thickness of the circle's outline.

fill → (int, "string", "#hex" or (red, green, blue) ) [optional]: Defines the background color of the arc. It is transparent by default.

</> Python

```
from PIL import Image, ImageDraw

arc  = Image.new(mode="RGB", size=(500,500), color="#3A6EA5")
draw = ImageDraw.Draw(im=arc)
draw.arc(xy= (50, 50, 350, 350), start=10, end=150, width= 10, fill="#EBEBEB")

arc.show()
```

chord(xy, start, end, width, fill, outline)

The chord() method draws an arc whose ends are connected by a line.

xy → (x, y) [required]: Defines the center coordinates of the circle.

start , end → (float) [required]: Define the start and end angles of the arc.

width → (float) [optional]: Determines the thickness of the arc's outline.

fill → (int, "string", "#hex" or (red, green, blue)) [optional]: Defines the background color of the chord. It is transparent by default.

```
</> Python
from PIL import Image, ImageDraw

chord  = Image.new(mode="RGB", size=(500,500), color="#3A6EA5")
draw = ImageDraw.Draw(im=chord)
xy = (50, 50, 400, 400)
draw.chord(xy= xy, start= 10, end=200, width= 15, fill="#ff6700", outline="#0D2137")

chord.show()
```

polygon(xy, width, fill, outline)

The **polygon()** method is used to draw a polygon by connecting multiple coordinate points.

xy → ( [(x1, y1), (x2, y2), (x3, y3), ...]) [required]: – A list of coordinate points that define the vertices of the polygon.

width → (float) [optional]: Determines the thickness of the polygon's outline.

fill → (int, "colorname", "#hex" or (red, green, blue)) [optional]: Defines the background color of the polygon. It is transparent by default.

</> Python

```
from PIL import Image, ImageDraw

poly  = Image.new(mode="RGB", size=(500,500), color="#3A6EA5")
draw = ImageDraw.Draw(im=poly)
xy = [(150, 450),(350, 450),(450, 250),(250, 50),(50, 250),]
draw.polygon(xy= xy, width= 10, outline="#ebebeb")

poly.show()
```

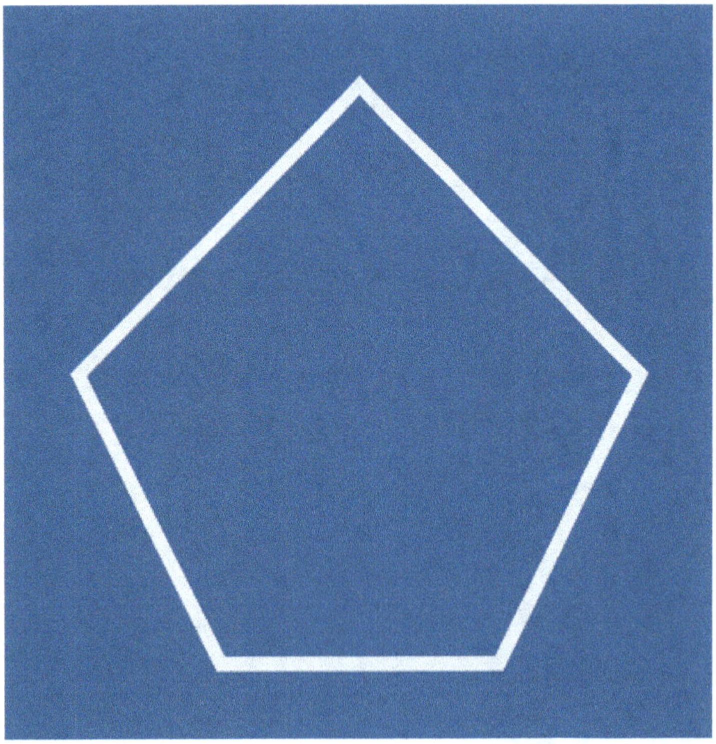

 

# The ImageEnhance Module

The **ImageEnhance** module provides various classes for enhancing images by adjusting their **color**, **contrast**, **brightness**, and **sharpness**. These classes take an image as a parameter and modify its appearance using an enhancement factor, typically ranging from **0.0** to **1.0**, where **1.0** represents the original image.

**Methods** — Pillow (PIL)

| Brightness | Contrast | ImageFilter | Sharpness |
|---|---|---|---|
| Color | Image | ImageStat | annotations |

**Deep**

To explore the available methods and attributes of the **ImageEnhance** module, use the dir() function.

```
>>> from PIL import  ImageEnhance
>>> dir(ImageEnhance)
```

The ImageEnhance module provides **three key objects** for each enhancement class:

**image**
Represents the input image and provides methods for manipulation and data retrieval.

**degenerate**
This generates the **least enhanced version** of the image, often used as a reference for scaling enhancements.

**enhance(factor)**
Applies the enhancement effect to the image based on the specified factor, where 1.0 represents the original image.

 

## Brightness(image)

The **Brightness()** class controls the light intensity of an image:

- A factor of **0.0** results in a completely dark image.
- A factor of **1.0** preserves the original brightness.
- A factor above **1.0** increases the brightness.

```python
from PIL import Image, ImageDraw
img  = Image.open("girl.jpeg")
enhanced1 = ImageEnhance.Brightness(image=img).enhance(factor=0.3)
enhanced2 = ImageEnhance.Brightness(image=img).enhance(factor=2)
enhanced3 = ImageEnhance.Brightness(image=img).enhance(factor=5)

img.show()
enhanced1.show()
enhanced2.show()
enhanced3.show()
```

*Original image*

*brightness factor: 0.3*

 | 

*brightness factor: 2*

*brightness factor : 5*

## Contrast(image)

The **Contrast()** class adjusts the difference between the darkest and lightest parts of an image:

- 📌 A factor of **0.0** results in a completely gray image.
- 📌 A factor of **1.0** maintains the original contrast.
- 📌 A factor above **1.0** increases contrast.

</> **Python**

```
from PIL import Image, ImageDraw
img  = Image.open("girl.jpeg")
img.show()
ImageEnhance.Contrast(image=img).enhance(factor=0.6).show()
ImageEnhance.Contrast(image=img).enhance(factor=2) .show()
ImageEnhance.Contrast(image=img).enhance(factor=4) .show()
```

*original image*

*contrast factor : 0.6*

*contrast factor : 2*

*contrast factor : 4*

 

## Color(image)

The **Color()** class manages the **saturation** or **intensity** of colors in an image:

- A factor of **0.0** converts the image to black and white.
- A factor of **1.0** keeps the original colors.
- A factor above **1.0** increases color vibrancy.

```python
from PIL import Image, ImageDraw
img  = Image.open("parrot.jpeg")
enhanced1 = ImageEnhance.Color(image=img).enhance(factor=0.
enhanced2 = ImageEnhance.Color(image=img).enhance(factor=0.4)
enhanced3 = ImageEnhance.Color(image=img).enhance(factor=3)

img.show()
enhanced1.show()
enhanced2.show()
enhanced3.show()
```

Original image

color factor : 0.0

color factor : 0.4

color factor : 3.0

## Sharpness(image)

The **Sharpness()** class controls the **clarity of edges and fine details** in an image:

- 📌 A factor of **0.0** results in a completely blurred image.
- 📌 A factor of **1.0** maintains the original sharpness.
- 📌 A factor above **1.0** enhances the sharpness.

</> Python

```python
from PIL import Image, ImageDraw
img  = Image.open("snow_trip.jpeg")
img.show()
ImageEnhance.Sharpness(image=img).enhance(factor= -10.0 ).show()
ImageEnhance.Sharpness(image=img).enhance(factor= 0.0) .show()
ImageEnhance.Sharpness(image=img).enhance(factor=15.0) .show()
```

*Original image*

*sharpness factor : -10.0*

*sharpness factor : 0.0*

*sharpness factor : 15.0*

 

# The ImageFilter Module

Image filtering enhances an image's appearance by modifying pixel values using predefined functions. The ImageFilter module in PIL provides various classes for applying different filtering effects.

**Predefined Filters in Pillow**

Pillow includes several built-in filters:

| Filter Name | Effect |
|---|---|
| SMOOTH | Applies a subtle smoothing effect |
| SMOOTH_MORE | Enhances the smoothing effect |
| BLUR | Softens the image |
| SHARPEN | Enhances image sharpness |
| FIND_EDGES | Highlights edges in the image |
| CONTOUR | Creates a contour-like effect |
| DETAIL | Enhances fine details |
| EDGE_ENHANCE | Enhances image edges |
| EDGE_ENHANCE_MORE | Stronger edge enhancement |
| EMBOSS | Creates an embossed effect |

*Table 5.3: Predefined Filters*

## Deep

To explore the available methods and attributes of the **ImageFilter** module, use the dir() function.

```
>>> from PIL import  ImageFilter
>>> dir(ImageFilter)
[........]
>>>
```

 

```python
from PIL import Image, ImageFilter
img  = Image.open("orange_love.png")
img.show()
img.filter( ImageFilter.BLUR ).show()
img.filter( ImageFilter.CONTOUR ).show()
img.filter( ImageFilter.SMOOTH_MORE ).show()
img.filter( ImageFilter.EMBOSS ).show()
img.filter( ImageFilter.FIND_EDGES ).show()
img.filter( ImageFilter.DETAIL ).show()
img.filter( ImageFilter.SHARPEN ).show()
```

Original image

BLUR

CONTOUR

SMOOTH_MORE

EMBOSS

FIND_EDGES

DETAIL

SHARPEN

## ImageFilter Classes

### RankFilter( size, rank)

Sorts all pixels in a window of the specified size and returns the rankth value.
size → (int)[required]: The kernel size in pixels.
rank → (int)[required]: The pixel value to pick.

- 0 → Minimum filter
- size*size/2 → Median filter
- size*size - 1 → Maximum filter

 

```python
from PIL import Image, ImageFilter
img  = Image.open("orange_love.png")
img.filter( ImageFilter.RankFilter( size = 7, rank= 2) ).show()
```

MinFilter(size)

Selects the lowest pixel value in a given window size.

size → (int)[required]: Kernel size in pixels.

MaxFilter(size)

Selects the highest pixel value in a given window size.

size → (int)[required]: Kernel size in pixels.

MedianFilter(size)

Selects the median pixel value in a given window size.

size → (int)[required]: Kernel size in pixels.

 

### ModeFilter(size)

Selects the most frequent pixel value in a given window size. Pixels that appear only once or twice are ignored.
size → (int)[required]: Kernel size in pixels.

### MultibandFilter

Used for filtering multi-band images.

### BoxBlur(radius)

Blurs the image by averaging pixel values in a square box extending radius pixels in each direction.
radius → (float or list of floats)[required]: Defines the blur area.

- radius = 0 → No blur applied

</> Python

```python
from PIL import Image, ImageFilter
img  = Image.open("orange_love.png")
img.filter( ImageFilter.BoxBlur( radius = 10) ).show()
```

### GaussianBlur(radius)

Blurs the image using a Gaussian kernel approximation with extended box filters.
radius → (float or list of floats)[required]: Defines the standard deviation of the Gaussian kernel.

 

# The ImageChops Module

The **ImageChops** module in Pillow provides a collection of channel operations ("chops") for performing arithmetic image manipulations. These operations are useful for image comparison, blending, masking, and logical operations.

Methods — Pillow (PIL)

| add | composite | duplicate | logical_and |
|---|---|---|---|
| add_modulo | constant | hard_light | logical_or |
| annotations | darker | invert | logical_xor |
| blend | difference | lighter | multiply |
| offset | overlay | screen | soft_light |
| subtract | subtract_modulo | | |

Deep

Use the dir() function to explore the available methods and attributes of the ImageChops module.

```
>>> from PIL import  ImageChops
>>> dir(ImageChops)
[........]
>>>
```

add( image1, image2, scale, offset )

This method **adds** one image to another with an optional **scale** and **offset**.

image1→ (PIL.Image) : First image.

image2 → (PIL.Image): Second image.

scale → (float)[optional- default=1.0]: The resulting image is divided by this scale factor.

offset → (int)[optional- default=0]: A value added to the result to adjust brightness.

 

```python
from PIL import Image, ImageChops

img1 = Image.open("freshview.jpeg")
img2 = Image.open("warmview.jpeg")
img1.show()
img2.show()
ImageChops.add(image1=img1, image2=img2, scale=3, offset=10).show()
```

### add_modulo( image1, image2, scale, offset )

This method **adds** two images without applying a scale factor, meaning pixel values wrap around (modulo 256).

image1→ (PIL.Image) : First image.

image2→ (PIL.Image) : Second image.

◇ **Use Case**: Prevents image values from clipping when they exceed the maximum pixel value.

### subtract( image1, image2, scale, offset )

Subtracts image2 from image1 and divides by a **scale** factor, with an optional **offset**.

image1 → (PIL.Image): First image.

image2 → (PIL.Image): Second image.

scale → (float)[optional- default=1.0]: Controls the degree of subtraction.

offset → (int)[optional- default=0]: Adjusts the resulting image brightness.

◇ **Use Case**: Used to detect changes between images.

</> Python

```
from PIL import Image, ImageChops

img1 = Image.open("freshview.jpeg")
img2 = Image.open("warmview.jpeg")
img = ImageChops.subtract(image1=img1, image2=img2, scale=3, offset=10)
img.save("new_image.jpg")
```

### subtract_modulo( image1, image2 )

Subtracts image2 from image1 without clipping pixel values (wraps around if values go negative).

image1→ (PIL.Image): First image.

image2→ (PIL.Image): Second image.

◇ **Use Case**: Works well for periodic images where wrapping pixel values is desired.

 

difference( image1, image2 )

Computes the **absolute difference** between two images, pixel by pixel.

◇ **Use Case**: Commonly used in image comparison and detecting changes between two images.

```python
from PIL import Image, ImageChops
img1 = Image.open("girl_with_orange.jpeg")
img2 = Image.open("girl_with_glass.jpeg")
img1.show()
img2.show()
ImageChops.difference(image1=img1, image2=img2).show()
```

### lighter( image1, image2 )

Creates an image where each pixel is the **lighter** value of the two images.

- **Use Case**: Useful for highlighting bright areas.

```python
from PIL import Image, ImageChops
img1 = Image.open("girl_with_orange.jpeg")
img2 = Image.open("girl_with_glass.jpeg")
ImageChops.lighter(image1=img1, image2=img2).show()
```

### hard_light( image1, image2 )

This method applies the **Hard Light** blending mode, which enhances contrast by either multiplying or screening the pixel values of two images based on the brightness of the top image.

- **Use Case**: Used for adding dramatic lighting effects by intensifying highlights and shadows

```python
img1 = Image.open("girl_with_orange.jpeg")
img2 = Image.open("girl_with_glass.jpeg")
ImageChops.hard_lighter(image1=img1, image2=img2).show()
```

 | 

### invert( image )

This method **inverts** an image, meaning dark areas become bright and vice versa.

- **Use Case**: Used for negative effects.

</> Python

```
img = Image.open("dark_girl.jpeg")
img.show()
ImageChops.invert(image = img).show()
```

multiply(image1, image2)

Multiplies pixel values of two images, making dark areas **darker** and bright areas **brighter**.

image1→ (PIL.Image): First image.

image2→ (PIL.Image): Second image.

- **Use Case**: Often used for shadow effects.

screen(image1, image2)

This method **blends two inverted images** and superimposes them.

image1→ (PIL.Image) – First image.

image2→ (PIL.Image) – Second image.

- **Use Case**: Used in graphics editing for soft light effects.

overlay(image1, image2)

Applies the **Overlay blending mode**, enhancing contrast by mixing highlights and shadows.

image1→ (PIL.Image): First image.

image2→ (PIL.Image): Second image.

- **Use Case**: Used in photo filters and color correction.

blend(image1, image2, alpha)

Blends two images with a constant **transparency weight** (alpha).

image1→ (PIL.Image): First image.

image2→ (PIL.Image): Second image.

alpha→ (float)[required]: A value between 0.0 (fully transparent) and 1.0 (fully visible).

- **Use Case**: Used in fading effects.

constant(image1, image2, value)

This method fills a channel with a given **gray level**.

image1→ (PIL.Image): First image.

image2→ (PIL.Image): Second image.

value → (int)[required]: Level of gray (0-255).

- **Use Case**: Used for background manipulation.

 

# The ImageGrab Module

The **ImageGrab** module in Pillow is primarily used for capturing screenshots of the entire computer screen or retrieving content from the clipboard. It provides two key functions: one for taking screenshots and another for extracting clipboard content.

## Taking Screenshots

grab( bbox, include_layered_window, all_screens, xdisplay )

The **grab()** function captures a screenshot of the screen. If no bounding box (bbox) is specified, it captures the entire screen.

bbox → (tuple)[optional]: Defines the region of the screen to capture in the format (x, y, width, height).

x, y → Coordinates of the top-left corner.

width, height → Dimensions of the region to capture.

include_layered_windows → (bool)[optional]: If True, captures layered windows (Windows-only).

all_screens → (bool)[optional]: If True, captures all screens in a multi-monitor setup (Windows-only).

xdisplay → (string): Specifies the display to capture (Linux-only).

</> Python

```python
from PIL import Image, ImageGrab

img  = ImageGrab.grab()
img.show()
img.save("screenshot.png")
```

 

## Capturing Clipboard Content

### grabclipboard()

The **grabclipboard()** function retrieves the current clipboard content if available.

**Return Values:**

- If an image is stored in the clipboard, it returns a PIL.Image object.
- If file paths are stored, it returns a list of filenames.
- Returns None if the clipboard is empty or contains unsupported data.

</> Python

```python
from PIL import Image, ImageGrab

content  = ImageGrab.grabclipboard()
print( content )
```

**Think about it ?**

1. Is there any other class in the ImageGrab module besides grab() and grabclipboard()?
2. How does the computer's print screen function differ from ImageGrab.grab()?

 

# Chapter Summary

Pillow, a fork of the Python Imaging Library (PIL), is a powerful Python module for creating, manipulating, enhancing, and transforming images. It provides numerous classes, each offering various methods and attributes for applying image effects. Some of the most commonly used classes include:

**Key Classes in Pillow**

Image Class

- Creating new images.
- Opening and loading existing images.
- Cropping, copying, and pasting images.
- Transforming images (resizing, rotating, etc.).
- Retrieving image attributes (size, mode, format, etc.).

ImageChops (Channel Operations)

- Differentiating between images.
- Inverting images.
- Blending multiple images.
- Performing logical operations to compare images.

ImageFilter

- Smoothing images.
- Detecting contours.
- Enhancing details.
- Highlighting edges.
- Sharpening images.

ImageEnhance

- Adjusting brightness.
- Modifying contrast levels.
- Controlling sharpness (blurring or sharpening).
- Increasing or decreasing color intensity and saturation.

ImageDraw

- Drawing shapes (lines, circles, rectangles, polygons, etc.).
- Writing text onto images.

ImageGrab

- Capturing screenshots.
- Copying clipboard content into an image.

**Importance of the Image Class**

The Image class is the foundation of Pillow and is often required before using other classes. It provides multiple ways to load or create images:

- new() – Creates an image from scratch.
- open() – Opens an existing image file.
- frombytes() – Loads an image from memory as bytes.

## Chapter Summary

The save() method is crucial for preserving modifications and converting between file formats. Each image format (e.g., GIF, JPEG, PNG) may require different parameters; for instance, GIF supports duration and loop, which are irrelevant for JPEG.

Additionally, changes can be previewed without saving by using the show() method, which opens a temporary version of the edited image in the system's default viewer.

Pillow is an essential library for image processing in Python, providing a comprehensive set of tools for various image manipulation tasks.

### Keywords

| | | | | |
|---|---|---|---|---|
| contrast | vibrancy | contour | radius | transverse |
| sharpness | outline | edges | rotation | mask |
| invert | chord | clockwise | transpose | clipboard |
| clipping | ellipse | blend | kernel | Multi-band |
| blurring | histogram | emboss | saturation | intensity |

### Discussion

1. What is Pillow, and how does it relate to the Python Imaging Library (PIL)?
2. Which core functionalities does the Image class provide, and why is it considered the most important class in Pillow?
3. How does the ImageChops module help in image processing, and in what scenarios would you use it?
4. What are the differences between ImageFilter and ImageEnhance, and how do they contribute to image modification?
5. How does the ImageDraw class allow for graphical modifications, and what are its practical applications
6. What is the purpose of ImageGrab, and how does it compare to the traditional print screen function?
7. How does the save() method in the Image class handle different image file formats, and why is it crucial for image processing?
8. What are the advantages of using show() instead of save() when previewing image modifications?
9. How can ImageEnhance be used to improve image quality, and what factors should be considered whe adjusting brightness, contrast, and sharpness?
10. In what ways can Pillow be used in real-world applications such as machine learning, graphic design, and automation?

# Review Questions

To which class does the open() method belong?
a. ImageDraw
b. ImageFont
c. Image
d. ImageEnhance

The brightness and sharpness of an image can be altered with:
a. ImageDraw
b. ImageFilter
c. ImageGrab
d. ImageEnhance

The RGB and L are kinds of:
a. Color band
b. Color mode
c. Pixel value
d. Channel

One of the following is an incorrect way to use color in PIL:
a. 256,
b. "green"
c. "156"
d. (200, 10, 20)

The RGB(0, 35, 0) will produce:
a. Violet
b. Blue
c. Red
d. Green

A color can be defined this way "#00334C":
a. True
b. False

Which module is used for taking snapshots of the current screen?
a. ImageGrab
b. ImageDraw
c. Image
d. ImageFilter

Which is NOT a filter in ImageFilter?
a. BLUR
b. CONTRAST
c. DETAIL
d. SMOOTH

9. Which one is NOT a valid image mode in Pillow?
   a. CYMK
   b. RGB
   c. L
   d. CMYK

10. The mandatory argument of the save() method is:
   a. Quality
   b. fp
   c. Loop
   d. Duration

11. In ImageDraw, the rectangle() method has the following parameters except:
   a. Xp
   b. Fill
   c. Radius
   d. Width

12. Choose the odd one out:
   a. Fill is a color parameter for border color
   b. Fill is a color parameter for background color
   c. Outline is a color parameter for border color
   d. Width is a float parameter for border thickness

13. The difference in parameters between rectangle and rounded_rectangle is:
   a. Width
   b. Radius
   c. Xp
   d. Fill

14. Which method can separate images into color bands?
   a. split()
   b. merge()
   c. mode()
   d. different()

15. The appropriate method for mode conversion is:
   a. merge()
   b. convert()
   c. save()
   d. transform()

16. append_images is a parameter of:
   a. show()
   b. save()
   c. split()
   d. open()

# Review Questions

17. Choose the odd one out:
    a. blend()
    b. blur()
    c. composite()
    d. darker()
18. The resize() method takes which of the following arguments?
    a. New size tuple
    b. Resampling filter
    c. Both a & b
    d. None of the above
19. Which module is used for image transformation like rotation and cropping?
    a. ImageDraw
    b. Image
    c. ImageGrab
    d. ImageEnhance
20. What function is used to create a blank image?
    a. new()
    b. blank()
    c. create()
    d. generate()

21. What does paste() do in the Image class?
    a. Overlays one image onto another
    b. Copies an image
    c. Saves an image
    d. Resizes an image
22. show() in PIL:
    a. Saves the image permanently
    b. Displays a temporary preview
    c. Converts the image mode
    d. Returns an image object
23. The default resampling filter for resizing an image is:
    a. BILINEAR
    b. NEAREST
    c. BOX
    d. LANCZOS
24. thumbnail() resizes an image while maintaining its:
    a. File format
    b. Aspect ratio
    c. Resolution
    d. Compression

25. Which module in PIL allows working with fonts?
    1. ImageFilter
    2. ImageDraw
    3. ImageFont
    4. ImageChops

26. What does rotate(90) do to an image?
    1. Flips the image
    2. Rotates 90 degrees counterclockwise
    3. Rotates 90 degrees clockwise
    4. Converts it to grayscale

27. How can you make an image grayscale?
    1. image.convert("L")
    2. image.filter(GRAYSCALE)
    3. image.apply_gray()
    4. image.gray()

28. What does transpose(FLIP_LEFT_RIGHT) do?
    1. Rotates the image 180 degrees
    2. Mirrors the image horizontally
    3. Flips the image vertically
    4. Converts it to grayscale

29. Which function merges multiple images into a single one?
    1. merge()
    2. blend()
    3. combine()
    4. composite()

30. The ImageEnhance.Contrast() function:
    1. Increases or decreases contrast
    2. Converts the image to grayscale
    3. Sharpens the image
    4. Reduces image size

31. What is the default format of Image.save() if no extension is given?
    1. PNG
    2. PPM
    3. JPEG

32. Which method finds the absolute difference betwee two images?
    a. ImageChops.difference()
    b. Image.filter()
    c. ImageEnhance()
    d. ImageDraw.line()

thon

cv2.imread()
cv2.imwrite()
cv2.line()
cv2.split()
dir(cv2)

# OpenCV (Open-source Computer Vision)

*After completing this chapter, you will be able to:*

- ☑ Understand the key features of OpenCV
- ☑ Explore essential methods and attributes
- ☑ Read and write images in various formats
- ☑ Perform geometric transformations on images
- ☑ Convert image colors between different spaces
- ☑ Apply filtering techniques to enhance images
- ☑ Utilize NumPy kernels for image processing
- ☑ Draw and manipulate shapes on images

# OpenCV

OpenCV is an open-source computer vision and image processing library used for tasks such as object detection, image recognition, machine learning, and real-time computer vision applications. The OpenCV library is available in multiple programming languages, including C++, Java, and MATLAB.

**Deep**

Open-source products, software, or source codes are free to use, modify, and customize. They do not require any fees for usage.

## Installing OpenCV in Python

To install OpenCV in Python, use the following command in the terminal or Command Prompt (Windows):

```
pip install opencv-python
```

## Key Features of OpenCV

| Feature | Function |
|---|---|
| ✅ **Image Processing** | • Filtering<br>• Transformations<br>• Edge detection<br>• Thresholding |

 

| | |
|---|---|
| ✅ **Object Detection and Tracking** | • Face detection<br>• Eye detection<br>• License plate detection<br>• Motion detection |
| ✅ **Machine Learning** | • Support Vector Machine (SVM)<br>• Deep learning with the DNN module |
| ✅ **Video Processing** | • Frame extraction<br>• Background subtraction<br>• Optical flow |
| ✅ **3D Vision** | • Stereo vision<br>• Depth estimation<br>• 3D reconstruction |
| ✅ **AI and Deep Learning** | • Integration with TensorFlow<br>• Integration with PyTorch |

*Table 6.0: Features of OpenCV*

### Note

This book focuses on the implementation of OpenCV for basic image processing. Other advanced functions, such as 3D vision, deep learning, and machine learning, are beyond the scope of this book.

### Deep

OpenCV images are stored as **NumPy** arrays in the form of matrices, where each pixel is represented as an element in the array.

 

# The CV2 Module

In Python, the OpenCV library is available as CV2, which can be imported directly into a program using the import statement:

```python
import cv2              # or
import cv2 as name      # Assigning an alias
```

## Basic Operation Methods

Methods — OpenCV

| | | | |
|---|---|---|---|
| imread | blur | cvtColor | findContours |
| imshow | boxFilter | GaussianBlur | fitEllipse |
| imwrite | boxPoints | Canny | fitLine |
| imresize | circle | threshold | flip |
| addText | clipLine | split | getAffineTransform |
| add | colorChange | line | getGaussianKernel |
| invert | compare | fillConvexPoly | getRotationMatrix2D |
| linearPolar | destroyWindow | stackBlur | getTextSize |
| medianBlur | detail | subtract | imcount |
| merge | detailEnhance | transform | imdecode |
| multiply | ellipse | transpose | imdecodemulti |
| polylines | ellipse2Poly | typing | imencode |
| putText | estimateAffine2D | waitKey | importlib |
| rectangle | estimateAffine3D | waitKeyEx | imread |
| reduce | estimateAffinePartial2D | warpAffine | imreadmulti |
| remap | invertAffineTransform | warpPerspective | imshow |
| resize | fillPoly | warpPolar | imwrite |
| rotate | filter2D | sepFilter2D | imwritemulti |

 

### Deep

Use dir(cv2) to get the entire list of methods provided by OpenCV.

```
>>> import cv2
>>> dir(cv2)
[........]
>>>
```

### waitKey(delay)

Determines the time in milliseconds to keep an image displayed before closing the window or until a key is pressed. If set to 0, the image remains in view until the user manually closes it.

### imread( filename, flags)

Loads an image with an option to change or preserve the color mode. By default, the image is opened in full screen, but flag values can control its size and mode.
filename: Specifies the image file to be read.
flags: Defines the color mode or resizing behavior.

**Color Modes:**

| Flag | Description |
|---|---|
| cv2.IMREAD_COLOR | Loads a color image |
| cv2.IMREAD_GRAYSCALE | Loads an image in grayscale |
| cv2.IMREAD_UNCHANGED | Loads the image as it is |
| cv2.IMREAD_ANYCOLOR | Loads the image in any available color format. |
| cv2.IMREAD_ANYDEPTH | Loads the image in its original bit depth |
| cv2.IMREAD_LOAD_GDAL | Loads image using Geospatial Data Abstraction Library |
| cv2.IMREAD_REDUCED_COLOR_2 | Loads a color image, reduced by a factor of 2 |
| cv2.IMREAD_REDUCED_COLOR_4 | Loads a color image, reduced by a factor of 4 |
| cv2.IMREAD_REDUCED_COLOR_8 | Loads a color image, reduced by a factor of 8 |
| cv2.IMREAD_REDUCED_GRAYSCALE_2 | Loads an image in grayscale, reduced by a factor of 2 |
| cv2.IMREAD_REDUCED_GRAYSCALE_4 | Loads an image in grayscale, reduced by a factor of 4 |
| cv2.IMREAD_REDUCED_GRAYSCALE_8 | Loads an image in grayscale, reduced by a factor of 8 |

*Table 6.1: OpenCV color flags*

 

```python
import cv2
img1 = cv2.imread("picture.jpg", flags= cv2.IMREAD_COLOR)
img2 = cv2.imread("picture.jpg", flags= 5)                    # using an integer instead
```

imshow( title, image)

Displays an image in a window with a specified title.

title: Window title.

image: Instance of imread().

```python
import cv2
img1 = cv2.imread("dog.jpg", flags= cv2.IMREAD_COLOR)
cv2.imshow("My Image", img1)

img2 = cv2.imread("dog.jpg", flags= cv2.IMREAD_GRAYSCALE)    # Loading grayscale
cv2.imshow("My Image", img2)
cv2.waitKey(0)
```

 | 

### destroyAllWindows( ) and destroyWindow( )

These functions are used to close all OpenCV windows that were opened using cv2.imshow(). It ensures that resources are properly released after displaying an image.

```python
import cv2

img1 = cv2.imread("image1.jpg", flags= cv2.IMREAD_ANYCOLOR)
img2 = cv2.imread("image.2jpg", flags= cv2.IMREAD_ANYCOLOR)

cv2.imshow("My First Image", img1)
cv2.imshow("My Second Image", img2)
cv2.waitKey(0)

cv2.destroyAllWindows( )            # releasing resources
```

### imwrite( filename, image)

Saves an edited image or converts it to another format.

filename: Name of the new image to be saved.

image: Processed image to be saved.

```python
import cv2
img = cv2.imread("image.jpg", flags= cv2.IMREAD_ANYCOLOR)
cv2.imwrite("newImage.png", img)
```

**Deep**

To convert an image from one format to another, simply change the file extension in the filename when saving the image.

```
>>> import  cv2
>>> img =  cv2.imread("image.ico", flags=2)
>>> cv2.imwrite( "newImage.png" , img)        # conversion from ICO to PNG
```

 

resize( image, size)

Resizes an image to a new width and height, either scaling it up or down.

image: The original image.

size: A tuple defining the new dimensions (width, height).

```python
import cv2
img = cv2.imread("good_boy.jpeg", flags= cv2.IMREAD_COLOR)
cv2.imshow("My Image", img)

resized = cv2.resize(img, (300, 400))
cv2.imshow("Resized Image", resized)
cv2.waitKey(0)
```

flip( src, flipCode, dst)

Flips an image vertically, horizontally, or both depending on the flip code.

src: The image to be flipped.

dst: (optional) Flipped image.

| Flip Codes | Direction |
|---|---|
| 0 | Vertical flip |
| 1 | Horizontal flip |
| -1 | Both directions |

*Table 6.2 : The flip codes*

Python

```
import cv2
img = cv2.imread("bright_girl.jpeg", flags= cv2.IMREAD_COLOR)
cv2.imshow("My Image", img)

flipped = cv2.flip(img, 0 )          # vertical flip
cv2.imshow("Vertical flipped", flipped)
cv2.imwrite("newImage.jpg", flipped)
cv2.waitKey(0)
```

Original image Vertical flip (0)

Horizontal flip(1)

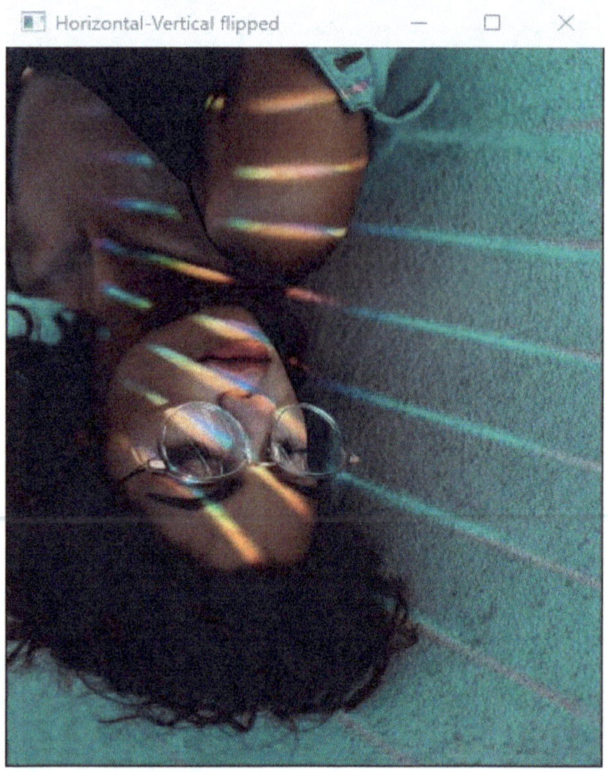

Both directions (-1)

rotate( src, rotateCode, dst)

Rotates an image about an axis with a specified rotation code.

src: The original image.

rotateCode: Defines the rotation angle.

dst: (optional) The rotated image

| Angles | Code | Rotation |
|---|---|---|
| cv2.ROTATE_90_CLOCKWISE | 0 | 90° clockwise |
| cv2.ROTATE_180 | 1 | 180° rotation |
| cv2.ROTATE_90_COUNTERCLOCKWISE | 2 | 270° or 90° counterclockwise |

*Table 6.3 : The rotate codes*

 

```python
import cv2
img = cv2.imread("bike.jpeg", flags= cv2.IMREAD_COLOR)
cv2.imshow("My Image", img)

rotated = cv2.rotate( img, 0 )          # 90º clockwise rotation
cv2.imshow("Rotaion", rotated)
cv2.waitKey(0)
cv2.destroyAllWindows()
```

Original image

90º (0) clockwise rotation

180º (1) rotation

90º or (2) counterclockwise rotation

 

### getRotationMatrix2D() and warpAffine()

In OpenCV, the **rotate()** method allows rotating an image only at predefined angles, such as 90°, 180°, and 270°. However, if you want to rotate an image at any user-specified angle, you need to use cv2.getRotationMatrix2D() along with cv2.warpAffine().

cv2.getRotationMatrix2D( center, angle, scale )

This method generates a 2D transformation matrix that serves as an input for the warpAffine() function to perform rotation.

center → (float, float): A tuple defining the center point around which the image rotates.
angle → (float): The rotation angle in degrees (0 to 360).
scale → (float): A scaling factor that determines if the image should be enlarged or reduced.

cv2.warpAffine( src, M, dsize, flags)

This method applies the rotation matrix from getRotationMatrix2D() to the image.

src → cv2.imread(): The source image to be transformed.
M → cv2.getRotationMatrix2D(): The transformation matrix.
dsize → (width, height): The dimensions of the output image.
flags → int or cv2.WARP_INVERSE_MAP: Specifies additional attributes like interpolation and mapping direction. Available flags include,

| | | |
|---|---|---|
| cv2.WARP_INVERSE_MAP | cv2.WARP_POLAR_LOG | cv2.WARP_POLAR_LINEAR |
| cv2.WARP_RELATIVE_MAP | cv2.WARP_FILL_OUTLIERS | cv2.INTER_LINEAR |

</> Python

```python
import cv2
img = cv2.imread("bike.jpeg", flags= cv2.IMREAD_REDUCED_COLOR_2)
cv2.imshow("My Image", img)

(h,w) = img.shape[:2]          # retrieving height and width of the image
center = (h//2, w//2)          # getting center of the image

matrix = cv2.getRotationMatrix2D(center= center, angle=45, scale=1 )
rotate = cv2.warpAffine(img, M=matrix, dsize=(h, w), borderMode=3, flags= 0)
cv2.imshow("Rotation", rotate)

cv2.waitKey(0)
cv2.destroyAllWindows()
```

### Deep

The **shape** attribute used above is a property of the image instance. There are several other properties available for working with image objects. To explore these properties, use the dir() function on the image object.

```
>>> import cv2
>>> img = imread("myImage.jpg", flags= cv2.IMREAD_COLOR)
>>> dir( img)
['all', 'any', 'argmax', 'argmin', 'argpartition', 'argsort', 'astype', 'base', 'byteswap', 'choose', 'clip', 'compress', 'conj', 'conjugate', 'copy', 'ctypes', 'cumprod', 'cumsum', 'data', 'device', 'diagonal', 'dot', 'dtype', 'dump', 'dumps', 'fill', 'flags', 'flat', 'flatten', 'getfield', 'imag', 'item', 'itemset', 'itemsize', 'mT', 'max', 'mean', 'min', 'nbytes', 'ndim', 'newbyteorder', 'nonzero', 'partition', 'prod', 'ptp', 'put', 'ravel', 'real', 'repeat', 'reshape', 'resize', 'round', 'searchsorted', 'setfield', 'setflags', 'shape', 'size', 'sort', 'squeeze', 'std', 'strides', 'sum', 'swapaxes', 'take', 'to_device', 'tobytes', 'tofile', 'tolist', 'tostring', 'trace', 'transpose', 'var', 'view']
>>>
```

 

## Cropping

OpenCV does not provide a built-in **crop()** function. However, cropping can be easily achieved using **NumPy slicing**.

### How Cropping Works

An image in OpenCV is represented as a **NumPy array**, so you can **crop** a specific region by defining the pixel range using:

```
cropped_img  = [y1:y2, x1:x2]
```

y1, x1 → The starting coordinates (top-left corner).

y2, x2 → The ending coordinates (bottom-right corner).

```python
import cv2
img = cv2.imread("flower.jpeg", flags= cv2.IMREAD_REDUCED_COLOR_2)
cv2.imshow("My Flower", img)

startX , startY =  50, 50          # starting point (x, y)
endX , endY =  330, 400          # ending point (x, y)

cropped_img = img[startY:endY, startX:endX ]
cv2.imshow("Cropping", cropped_img)

cv2.waitKey(0)
cv2.destroyAllWindows()
```

## Color Conversion

cvtColor(src, code, dst)

In OpenCV, the cvtColor() method is used to change the color space of an image. It converts an image from one color mode to another based on the specified conversion code.

src → imread() [required] : Specifies the image to be processed.
code → (int or cv2.COLOR_*) [required]: Defines the target color space for conversion.
dst → imread() [optional] : Processed image.

| Conversion Code | Description |
|---|---|
| cv2.COLOR_BGR2GRAY | Converts BGR image to Grayscale |
| cv2.COLOR_BGR2RGB | Converts BGR image to RGB |
| cv2.COLOR_BGR2HSV | Converts BGR image to HSV (Hue, Saturation, Value) |
| cv2.COLOR_BGR2LAB | Converts BGR image to LAB color space |

 

| cv2.COLOR_BGR2YCrCb | Converts BGR image to YCrCb color space |
|---|---|
| cv2.COLOR_BGR2XYZ | Converts BGR image to CIE XYZ color space |
| cv2.COLOR_BGR2HLS | Converts BGR image to HLS (Hue, Lightness, Saturation) |
| cv2.COLOR_BGR2LUV | Converts BGR image to LUV color space |
| cv2.COLOR_RGB2GRAY | Converts RGB image to Grayscale |
| cv2.COLOR_RGB2BGR | Converts RGB image to BGR |
| cv2.COLOR_RGB2HSV | Converts RGB image to HSV |
| cv2.COLOR_RGB2LAB | Converts RGB image to LAB |
| cv2.COLOR_RGB2YCrCb | Converts RGB image to YCrCb |
| cv2.COLOR_HSV2BGR | Converts HSV image to BGR |
| cv2.COLOR_HSV2RGB | Converts HSV image to RGB |

*Table 6.4 : OpenCV color conversion codes*

</> Python

```
import cv2
img = cv2.imread("flower.jpeg", flags= cv2.IMREAD_REDUCED_COLOR_2)
cv2.imshow("My Flower", img)

color_img = cv2.cvtColor(img, cv2.COLOR_RGB2GRAY)
cv2.imshow("Color conversion", color_img)
cv2.waitKey(0)
```

## Splitting and Merging Color Channels

### split(image)

The split() function separates an image into its individual color channels (B, G, R), each represented as a grayscale image.

image → imread() [required]: Specifies the image to be split.

```python
import cv2
img = cv2.imread("flower.jpeg", flags= cv2.IMREAD_REDUCED_COLOR_2)
color_bands = cv2.split(img)        # color_bands = (blue, green, red)
```

### merge([B, G, R])

The merge() function combines separate color channels back into a single image.

- **B**: image – Blue channel
- **G**: image – Green channel
- **R**: image – Red channel

```python
import cv2

img = cv2.imread("flower.jpeg", flags= cv2.IMREAD_REDUCED_COLOR_2)
cv2.imshow("My Flower", img)

color_bands = cv2.split(img)
red = color_bands[2]
green = color_bands[1]
blue = color_bands[0]

merge_image = cv2.merge([blue, green, red])
cv2.imshow("Merged images", merge_image)

cv2.waitKey(0)
cv2.destroyAllWindows()
```

Orignal image

cv2.merge([blue, green, red])

cv2.merge([red, green, blue])

cv2.merge([green, blue, red])

 

## Image Filtering

GaussianBlur(img, ksize, sigmaX, sigmaY)

The GaussianBlur() method applies a Gaussian filter to smooth or blur an image.

img → imread() [required]: The image to be blurred.

ksize → (x, y) [required] : Kernel size; both values should be odd numbers.

sigmaX → int [required]: Standard deviation in the X direction.

sigmaY → int [optional] : Standard deviation in the Y direction.

```python
import cv2
img = cv2.imread("smile_girl.jpg", flags= cv2.IMREAD_REDUCED_COLOR_2)
cv2.imshow("Smile", img)

blur_img = cv2.GaussianBlur(src=img, ksize=(5, 7), sigmaX=1)
cv2.imshow("Blur Image", blur_img)

cv2.waitKey(0)
cv2.destroyAllWindows()
```

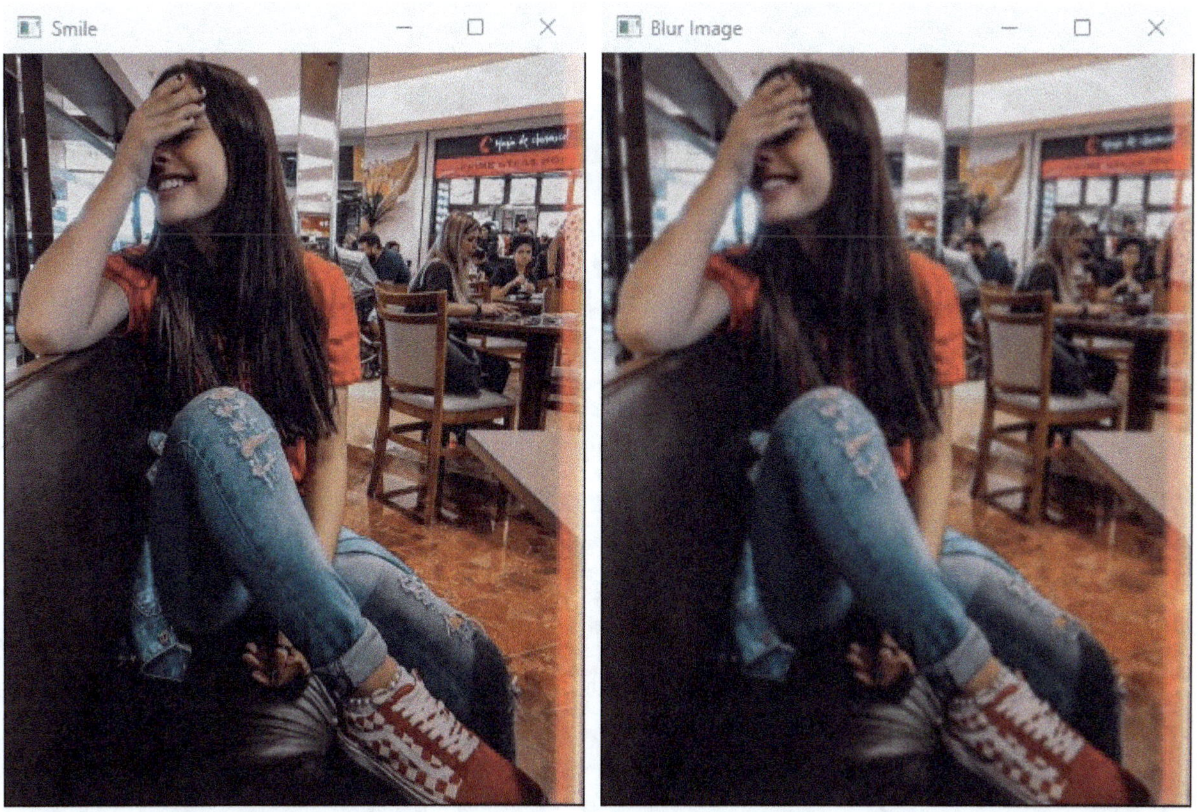


 

medianBlur(img, ksize)

The medianBlur() function is another method for blurring an image, using the median filter.

src → imread() [required]: The image to be blurred.

ksize →(int) [required] : Kernel size; must be an odd number.

```python
import cv2
img = cv2.imread("smile_girl.jpg", flags= cv2.IMREAD_REDUCED_COLOR_2)

blur_img = cv2.medianBlur(src=img, ksize= 5)
cv2.imwrite("newImage.jpg", blur_img)
```

# NumPy in OpenCV

NumPy is heavily used in OpenCV because it provides efficient array operations, which are essential for image processing, as images are represented as matrices.

OpenCV filter methods use a **kernel**, which is a NumPy array that defines how pixel values are modified. Each value in the kernel determines the influence of neighboring pixels on the output pixel.

### Understanding the Kernel

A **kernel (filter)** is a small matrix (e.g., 3×3, 5×5) that is convolved over an image to modify pixel values.

Example of a **sharpening kernel**:

 

| | | |
|---|---|---|
| 0 | -1 | 0 |
| -1 | 5 | -1 |
| 0 | -1 | 0 |

The **center pixel (5)** is multiplied by itself → increases its intensity (sharpens the pixel).

The **surrounding pixels (-1)** reduce their effect → enhances contrast.

The **sum of values is 1**, ensuring the image brightness remains preserved.

filter2D(src, ddepth, kernel, ...)
Applies a custom kernel to an image for sharpening, blurring, or edge detection.
src → imread(): Defines the source image.
ddepth → (int): Specifies the desired depth of the output image (-1 keeps the same depth as the input).
kernel → (array): Defines how each pixel is processed.

</> Python

```
import cv2
import numpy as np

img = cv2.imread("smile_girl.jpg", flags= cv2.IMREAD_REDUCED_COLOR_2)
cv2.imshow("Smile", img)

kernel = np.array([[0,-1, 0 ],      # sharpening kernel
                   [-1, 5, -1],
                   [0, -1, 0]])

sharpened_img = cv2.filter2D(src=img, ddepth= -1, kernel=kernel)
cv2.imshow("Sharpness", sharpened_img)

cv2.waitKey(0)
cv2.destroyAllWindows()
```

 | 

## Blurring with Box Filter

boxFilter(src, ddepth, ksize)
src → imread(): Defines the source image.
ddepth → int: Specifies the desired depth (-1 keeps the same depth as the input).
ksize → (x, y): Defines the kernel size.

```python
import cv2
img = cv2.imread("smile_girl.jpg", flags = cv2.IMREAD_REDUCED_COLOR_2)

new_img = cv2.boxFilter(src=img, ddepth= -1, ksize= (5, 6) )
cv2.imwrite("blurred_image.jpg", new_img)
```

 

## Adjusting Brightness & Contrast

convertScaleAbs(img, alpha, beta)
This method adjusts the light intensity or brightness of an image.
img → imread(): Defines the input image.
alpha → (float): **Controls contrast**. Higher values make bright areas brighter and dark areas darker.
beta → (float): **Adjusts brightness**. Positive values increase brightness, while negative values decrease brightness.

</> Python

```
import cv2
img = cv2.imread("eagle.png", flags= cv2.IMREAD_REDUCED_COLOR_2)
cv2.imshow("Eagle", img)

new_img = cv2.convertScaleAbs(src=img, alpha= 2.8, beta= 5)
cv2.imshow("Contrast and Brightness", new_img)
cv2.waitKey(0)
```

## Edge Detection in OpenCV

Canny(image, threshold1, threshold2)

The **Canny** method detects edges by scanning intensity gradients in an image.
image → imread(): Defines the input image.
threshold1 → (float): First threshold to detect weak edges.
threshold2 → (float): Second threshold to detect strong edges.

</> Python

```
import cv2
img = cv2.imread("flower.png", flags= cv2.IMREAD_REDUCED_COLOR_2)
cv2.imshow("Black Roses", img)

new_img = cv2.Canny(image=img, threshold1=100.0, threshold2=100.0)
cv2.imshow("Edge Detection", new_img)
cv2.waitKey(0)
```

## Drawing Shapes

putText( img, text, org, fontFace, fontScale, color, thickness, lineType )

The putText() method is used to embed text into an image.

img → (image): The image to write text on (loaded using cv2.imread()).

text → (string): The actual text string to be displayed.

org →(float, float): A tuple (x, y) specifying the coordinates for text placement.

fontface → Defines the font type. OpenCV provides predefined font styles.

fontscale → (float): Defines the enlargement factor of the text.

color → (float, float, float): The text color in **BGR** format (Blue, Green, Red).

thickness → (float): Defines the boldness of the text.

linetype → (int): Determines the text rendering style (cv2.LINE_8, cv2.LINE_4, cv2.LINE_AA).

Available Font Families

| Font Type | Description |
|---|---|
| cv2.FONT_HERSHEY_SIMPLEX | Normal sans-serif font. |
| cv2.FONT_HERSHEY_PLAIN | Small plain font. |
| cv2.FONT_HERSHEY_DUPLEX | Similar to SIMPLEX but slightly thicker. |
| cv2.FONT_HERSHEY_COMPLEX | More complex, slightly more artistic. |
| cv2.FONT_HERSHEY_TRIPLEX | Similar to COMPLEX but thicker. |
| cv2.FONT_HERSHEY_SCRIPT_SIMPLEX | Handwriting-style script font. |
| cv2.FONT_HERSHEY_SCRIPT_COMPLEX | More complex script-style font. |
| cv2.FONT_ITALIC | Can be combined with other fonts for italicized text. |

*Table 6.5 : Predefined font families*

</> Python

```python
import cv2
img = cv2.imread("nature.png", flags= cv2.IMREAD_ANYCOLOR)
cv2.imshow("Nature", img)

new_img = cv2.addText(img=img, text="life is good", org=(100, 200), color=(20, 50, 200 ),
fontFace=cv2.FONT_HERSHEY_SIMPLEX, fontScale=1, thickness=2, lineType=2 )

cv2.imshow("Add Text", new_img)
cv2.waitKey(0)
```

line(img, pt1, pt2, color, thickness, lineType)

The line() function draws a straight line between two points.

img → cv2.imread(): The image where the line will be drawn.

pt1 → (float, float): The starting point (x, y) of the line.

pt2 → (float, float): The ending point (x, y) of the line.

color → (float, float, float): Line color in BGR format (Blue, Green, Red).

thickness → (int) : Width of the line.

lineType → Defines the rendering style (cv2.LINE_8, cv2.LINE_4, cv2.LINE_AA).

</> Python

```python
import cv2
import numpy as np

img = np.zeros((300, 400, 3), dtype= np.uint8)        # creating an image with h:300, w:400
```

 

```
img[:] = (2,  20, 5)                                        # defining the image color

line = cv2.line(img=img, pt1=(50, 100), pt2=(350, 250), color=(250, 250, 250), thickness=5)
cv2.imshow("Line", line)
cv2.waitKey(0)
```

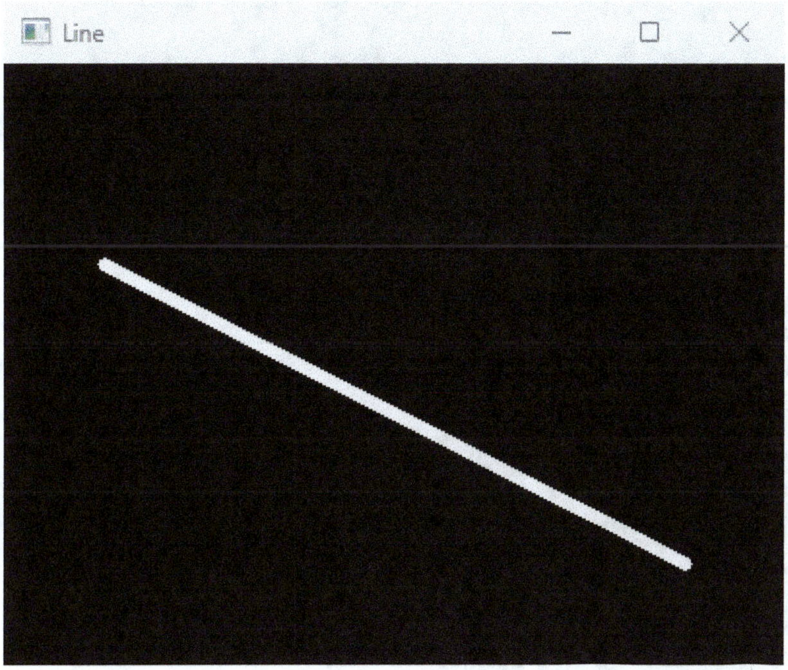


rectangle(img, rec, color, thickness, lineType)

The rectangle() method is used to draw a rectangle or square.

img → (cv2.imread): The image where the rectangle will be drawn.

rec→ (float, float,float,float): A tuple (x, y, width, height), where (x, y) is the top-left coordinate.

color →(float, float, float): Rectangle color in **BGR** format (Blue, Green, Red).

thickness → (float): Border thickness (use -1 to fill the rectangle).

lineType → The type of line (cv2.LINE_8, cv2.LINE_4, cv2.LINE_AA).

 

```python
import cv2
import numpy as np
img = np.zeros((300, 400, 3), dtype= np.uint8)      # creating an image with h:300, w:400
img[:] = (2,  20, 5)                                  # defining the image color

rectangle = cv2.rectangle(img=img, rec=(50, 50, 300, 200), color=(250, 250, 250),
thickness=5)
cv2.imshow("Line", rectangle)
cv2.waitKey(0)
```

circle(img, center, radius, color, thickness, lineType)

The circle() method is used to draw a circle with a specified radius.

img → (cv2.imread): The image where the circle will be drawn.

center → (float, float): A tuple (x, y) representing the center of the circle.

radius → (float): The radius of the circle.

color→ (float, float, float): Circle border color in **BGR** format (Blue, Green, Red).

 

thickness → (int): Border thickness (use -1 to fill the circle).
linetype → The line rendering style (cv2.LINE_8, cv2.LINE_4, cv2.LINE_AA).

```python
import cv2
import numpy as np
img = np.zeros((300, 400, 3), dtype= np.uint8)      # creating an image with h:300, w:400
img[:] = (2,  20, 5)                                 # defining the background color

circle = cv2.circle(img=img, center=(200, 150), radius=100, color=(250, 250, 250),
thickness=5)

cv2.imshow("Circle", circle)
cv2.waitKey(0)
```

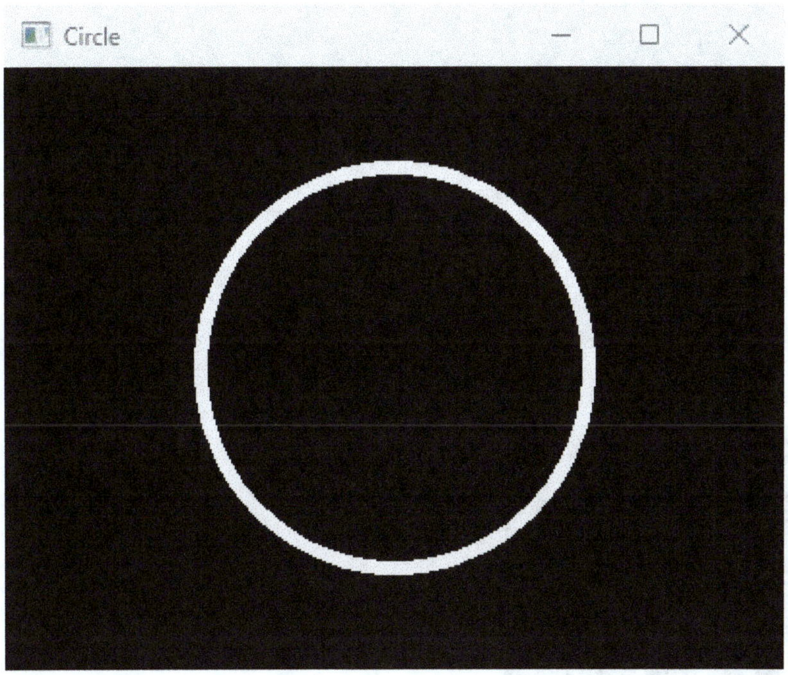


 

ellipse(img, center, axes, angle, startAngle, endAngle, color, thickness, lineType)

The ellipse() method is used to draw an elliptical shape with a specified center, axes, and angles.

img → (cv2.imread): The image where the ellipse will be drawn.
center → (float, float): A tuple (x, y) representing the center of the ellipse.
axes → (float, float): A tuple (major-axis, minor-axis) defining the size of the ellipse.
angle → (float): The rotation angle of the ellipse in degrees.
startAngle → (int): The starting angle of the arc (in degrees).
endAngle → (int): The ending angle of the arc (in degrees).
color → (float, float, float): The color of the ellipse outline.
thickness → (int) : Border thickness (use -1 to fill the ellipse).
lineType → The line rendering style (cv2.LINE_8, cv2.LINE_4, cv2.LINE_AA).

</> Python

```python
import cv2
import numpy as np
img = np.zeros((300, 400, 3), dtype= np.uint8)      # creating an image with h:300, w:400
img[:] = (2,  20, 5)                                # defining the background color

ellipse = cv2.ellipse(img=img, center=(200, 100), axes= (130,130) , angle=360,
startAngle=180, endAngle=0,  color=(250, 250, 250), thickness=3)

cv2.imshow("Ellipse", ellipse)
cv2.waitKey(0)
```

polylines(img, pts, isClosed, color, thickness, lineType)

The polylines() method allows drawing of multiple connected lines to form a polygon.

img → (cv2.imread): The image where the shape will be drawn.
pts → A list of points [(x1, y1), (x2, y2), ...] defining the shape.
isClosed → (bool): A boolean (True for a closed shape, False for an open shape).
color → (float, float, float): Shape color in **BGR** format (Blue, Green, Red).
thickness → (int) : The thickness of the lines.
lineType → The line rendering style (cv2.LINE_8, cv2.LINE_4, cv2.LINE_AA).

```python
import cv2
import numpy as np
img = np.zeros((300, 400, 3), dtype= np.uint8)       # creating an image with h:300, w:400
img[:] = (2,  20, 5)                                 # defining the background color

points = np.array([[100, 150], [200, 50], [300, 150], [250, 250], [150, 250]], np.int32)
points = points.reshape((-1, 1, 2))

polylines = cv2.polylines(img=img, pts= [points], isClosed= True,  color=(250, 250, 250),
thickness=3)
cv2.imshow("Polylines", polylines)

cv2.waitKey(0)
```

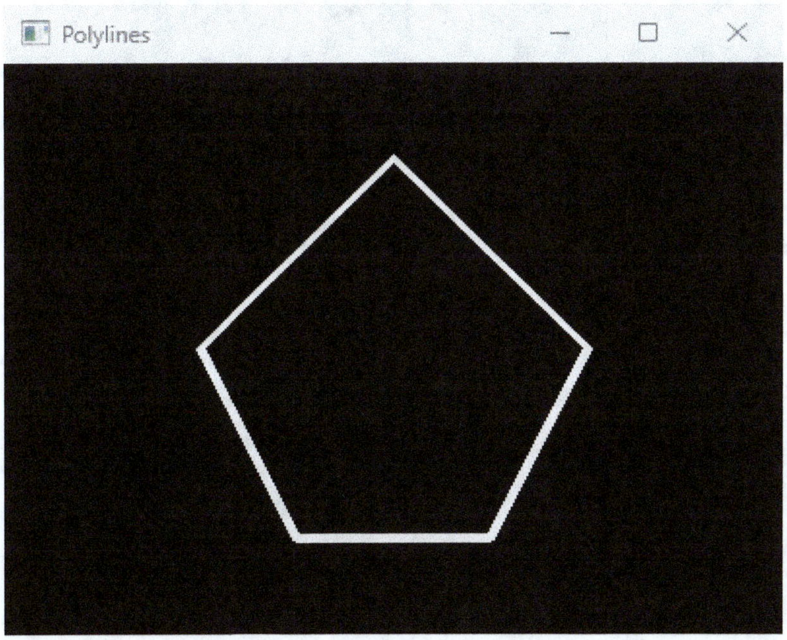


 

copyMakeBorder(src, top, bottom, left, right, borderType, value)

The copyMakeBorder() function is used to create a border around an image.

src → (cv2.imread): The input image to apply the border.

top, bottom, left, right → (int): Number of pixels to add to each side.

borderType → (int or border) : The type of border. The available border types include

| cv2.BORDER_CONSTANT | cv2.BORDER_DEFAULT | cv2.BORDER_REFLECT |
|---|---|---|
| cv2.BORDER_REPLICATE | cv2.BORDER_ISOLATE | cv2.BORDER_TRANSPARENT |
| cv2.BORDER_WRAP | cv2.BORDER_REFLECT101 | cv2.BORDER_REFLECT_101 |

value → BGR (float, float, float): The color of the border (used when borderType = cv2.BORDER_CONSTANT).

```
</> Python
import cv2
img = cv2.imread("puppy.jpg", flags=cv2.IMREAD_REDUCED_COLOR_2)
cv2.imshow("Puppy", img)

border = cv2.copyMakeBorder(src=img, top=30, bottom=30, left=30, right=30,
borderType= cv2.BORDER_REPLICATE, value=(10,0,50) )
cv2.imshow("Image with Border", border)
cv2.waitKey(0)
```

## Chapter Summary

OpenCV provides various functions for image processing, with **NumPy** playing a crucial role since images are represented as NumPy arrays. NumPy enables efficient matrix operations, which are essential for transformations, filtering, and analysis.

- **Image Rotation & Cropping**: getRotationMatrix2D() and warpAffine() allow rotation at custom angles, while cropping is handled using NumPy array slicing (img[y1:y2, x1:x2]).
- **Color Conversion**: cvtColor() changes an image's color mode, and split()/merge() manage individual color channels.
- **Image Filtering & Sharpening**: Techniques like GaussianBlur() and medianBlur() smooth images, while kernel-based filtering sharpens them. NumPy defines kernels used in these operations.
- **Edge Detection**: Canny() detects edges using threshold values.
- **Drawing Shapes**: Functions like line(), rectangle(), circle(), and polylines() allow drawing on images.
- **Creating New Images**: NumPy enables creating blank images using arrays, which can be modified with OpenCV functions.

## Keywords

kernel, hue, alpha, sigmaY, flip
matrix, saturation, beta, grayscale, slicing
Canny, threshold, sigmaX, array

## Discussion

1. How does NumPy contribute to image processing in OpenCV?
2. What are the differences between getRotationMatrix2D() and OpenCV's built-in rotate() method?
3. How can we efficiently crop an image using OpenCV without a predefined function?
4. What are the different color conversion codes available in OpenCV, and how are they used?
5. How do convolutional kernels work in image filtering and sharpening?
6. What are the key differences between Gaussian blur, median blur, and box filtering?
7. How does edge detection using Canny() differ from other edge detection methods?
8. What are the advantages of using polylines() instead of drawing individual shapes?
9. Why is convertScaleAbs() useful in adjusting image brightness, and how does it differ from direct pixel manipulation?
10. How can OpenCV be integrated with deep learning models for advanced image processing tasks?

# Review Questions

1. What does OpenCV primarily deal with?
   a) Video editing
   b) Image processing
   c) Audio processing
   d) Data analysis
2. Which library is used in OpenCV for handling arrays and matrices?
   a) Pandas
   b) NumPy
   c) Matplotlib
   d) Scipy
3. What function is used to read an image in OpenCV?
   a) cv2.imread()
   b) cv2.readImage()
   c) cv2.loadImage()
   d) cv2.openImage()
4. Which method is used to display an image?
   a) cv2.showImage()
   b) cv2.imshow()
   c) cv2.display()
   d) cv2.viewImage()
5. Which method is used to write an image to disk?
   a) cv2.write()
   b) cv2.saveImage()
   c) cv2.imwrite()
   d) cv2.exportImage()
6. What does cv2.cvtColor() do?
   a) Changes image brightness
   b) Converts an image to grayscale
   c) Converts an image's color space
   d) Blurs an image
7. Which method is used to rotate an image at a user-defined angle?
   a) cv2.rotate()
   b) cv2.getRotationMatrix2D() + cv2.warpAffine()
   c) cv2.transform()
   d) cv2.imageRotate()
8. What does cv2.resize() do?
   a) Converts the image to grayscale
   b) Increases image sharpness
   c) Changes the dimensions of an image
   d) Removes background
9. Which OpenCV method is used to crop an image?
   a) cv2.crop()
   b) cv2.imageCut()
   c) Slicing using NumPy (img[y1:y2, x1:x2])
   d) cv2.trim()
10. Which OpenCV function is used to apply geometric transformations?
    a) cv2.affineTransform()
    b) cv2.warpAffine()
    c) cv2.perspectiveTransform()
    d) cv2.shapeTransform()
11. Which filter is best suited for reducing noise while preserving edges?
    a) Gaussian Blur
    b) Median Blur
    c) Box Filter
    d) Bilateral Filter
12. Which method applies a sharpening effect using a kernel?
    a) cv2.sharpen()
    b) cv2.filter2D()
    c) cv2.smooth()
    d) cv2.imageSharp()
13. What is the purpose of using convertScaleAbs() in OpenCV?
    a) To perform image scaling and normalization
    b) To convert an image to grayscale
    c) To detect edges in an image
    d) To apply a threshold to an image
14. Which function is used for edge detection in OpenC
    a) cv2.edgeDetect()
    b) cv2.findEdges()
    c) cv2.Canny()
    d) cv2.edgeFilter()
15. Which parameter in the cv2.Canny() function determines the strong edges?
    a) Threshold1
    b) Threshold2
    c) Kernel size
    d) Depth
16. Which OpenCV function is used to detect contours i image?
    a) cv2.findContours()
    b) cv2.detectEdges()
    c) cv2.contourDetect()
    d) cv2.contourFind()

```
thon
pip install  imageio
import image.v2 as im
dir(im)
im.imread('path/image')
im.write('new.jpg', img)
```

# ImageIO

*After completing this chapter, you will be able to:*

- ☑ Understand the methods and attributes of ImageIO
- ☑ Read image files using ImageIO
- ☑ Write image files in different formats
- ☑ Explore the attributes and properties of a read image
- ☑ Convert image files to various formats efficiently

# ImageIO

**ImageIO** is a powerful Python library designed for reading and writing image data in various formats. While it primarily serves as an input/output library, it includes several useful functions that support image processing tasks.

## Installing ImageIO

To install the ImageIO library, follow the standard Python package installation method using pip:

```
pip install imageio
```

This installation process is similar to installing OpenCV or other Python libraries.

### Methods and Attributes in ImageIO

**Methods** ImageIO

| | | | |
|---|---|---|---|
| config | get_writer | imread | mimread |
| core | help | imread_v2 | mimsave |
| formats | imiter | imsave | mimwrite |
| get_reader | imopen | imwrite | mvolread |
| mvolsave | plugins | show_formats | v2 |
| mvolwrite | read | typing | v3 |
| volread | volsave | volwrite | warnings |

 

## Reading and Writing Images

### imread(uri)

Reads an image file of any format.

uri → (string) = "image.jpg" or "path/to/image.jpg": Specifies the filename or path of the image to be read.

```python
import imageio.v2 as image

img = image.imread("myImage.png")
```

**Deep**

The imageio.imread() class includes various methods and attributes for working with read images. The dir() function can be used to explore these available methods and attributes.

```
>>> import imageio
>>> img = imageio.imread("myImage.jpg")
>>> dir(img)
['all', 'any', 'argmax', 'argmin', 'argpartition', 'argsort', 'astype', 'base', 'byteswap', 'choose', 'clip', 'compress', 'conj', 'conjugate', 'copy', 'ctypes', 'cumprod', 'cumsum', 'data', 'device', 'diagonal', 'dot', 'dtype', 'dump', 'dumps', 'fill', 'flags', 'flat', 'flatten', 'getfield', 'imag', 'item', 'itemset', 'itemsize', 'mT', 'max', 'mean', 'min', 'nbytes', 'ndim', 'newbyteorder', 'nonzero', 'partition', 'prod', 'ptp', 'put', 'ravel', 'real', 'repeat', 'reshape', 'resize', 'round', 'searchsorted', 'setfield', 'setflags', 'shape', 'size', 'sort', 'squeeze', 'std', 'strides', 'sum', 'swapaxes', 'take', 'to_device', 'tobytes', 'tofile', 'tolist', 'tostring', 'trace', 'transpose', 'var', 'view']
>>>
```

 

imwrite(uri, im, format)

Writes a processed image to a file, also allowing format conversion.

uri → (string) = "new_image.png": Defines the filename for the saved image.

im → imread() : Specifies the image to be saved.

format → "PNG", "JPEG", "GIF", etc. [Optional]: Determines the output image format.

</> Python

```python
import imageio.v2 as image

img = image.imread("myImage.png")
image.imwrite("newImage.jpg", img)
```

**Think about it ?**

Is ImageIO primarily used for image file conversion, or does it offer additional functionalities for reading images?

 

# Chapter Summary

mageIO is a Python library designed for reading and writing images in various formats. It serves as an efficient tool for handling image files, supporting multiple formats like PNG, JPEG, and GIF. While its primary function is input and output operations, it also provides methods to facilitate image processing.

**Key Features:**

- **Installation:** Easily installed using pip install imageio.
- **Reading Images:** The imread() method loads images from a file or URL.
- **Writing Images:** The imwrite() method saves images in different formats.
- **Format Conversion:** Converts images between formats by specifying a new format in imwrite().
- **Exploring Methods:** The dir() function helps list available methods and attributes for further image manipulation.

Although ImageIO is mainly an I/O library, it integrates well with other image processing tools like OpenCV and NumPy, making it a versatile choice for handling image data in Python.

## Keywords

plugins

## Discussion

1. What are the key differences between ImageIO and OpenCV in terms of image handling?
2. How does ImageIO facilitate image format conversion?
3. What are the advantages of using ImageIO for reading and writing images?
4. In what scenarios would you choose ImageIO over other libraries like PIL or OpenCV?
5. How does ImageIO interact with NumPy for image processing tasks?
6. What are some common use cases of ImageIO in real-world applications?
7. How can you determine the available methods and attributes of an ImageIO object?
8. What are the limitations of ImageIO when it comes to advanced image processing?
9. How does ImageIO handle different image formats, and what challenges might arise?
10. Can ImageIO be integrated with other libraries for advanced image manipulation? If so, how?

## Review Questions

1. What is the primary function of ImageIO in Python?
   a) Image editing
   b) Image filtering
   c) Reading and writing image data
   d) Machine learning

2. Which command is used to install ImageIO?
   a) pip install opencv
   b) pip install imageio
   c) install imageio
   d) python install imageio

3. What method is used to read an image using ImageIO?
   a) imageio.read()
   b) imageio.open()
   c) imageio.imread()
   d) imageio.load()

4. What parameter is required in imageio.imread(uri)?
   a) Image filter type
   b) Image file name or path
   c) Image dimensions
   d) Image encoding format

5. How do you save an image using ImageIO?
   a) imageio.save()
   b) imageio.write()
   c) imageio.imwrite()
   d) imageio.store()

6. Which of the following is a valid format that Image supports for writing images?
   a) PDF
   b) PNG
   c) DOCX
   d) TXT

7. What function can be used to explore available methods and attributes in ImageIO?
   a) help(imageio)
   b) dir(imageio)
   c) methods(imageio)
   d) info(imageio)

8. Can ImageIO be used for image format conversion
   a) Yes
   b) No

9. ImageIO primarily deals with:
   a) Image transformations
   b) Image I/O operations
   c) Machine learning models
   d) Video processing

10. What additional library is commonly used with ImageIO for processing images as NumPy arrays?
    a) Pandas
    b) Matplotlib
    c) NumPy
    d) TensorFlow

```
import turtle
tut = turtle.Turtle()
tut.circle(100)
tut.shape("turtle")
tut.home()
tut.forward(50)
```

# Turtle

*After completing this chapter, you will be able to:*

- ☑ Understand various methods and attributes of the Turtle module
- ☑ Use Turtle for basic drawing operations
- ☑ Move and position the Turtle on the screen
- ☑ Apply pen control methods for drawing customization
- ☑ Modify the Turtle's appearance and shape
- ☑ Draw different geometric shapes using Turtle
- ☑ Control the screen and window settings for better visualization

# Turtle

The Python Turtle module is a powerful tool for drawing geometric shapes, animations, and patterns by moving the turtle (cursor) in different directions on the screen. The turtle follows a set of programmed instructions, allowing users to create intricate designs. This module is pre-packaged in Python and can be imported using the import turtle statement.

Turtle graphics are widely used in educational environments to introduce programming concepts in a fun and interactive way. It helps beginners understand loops, functions, and event-driven programming by visually representing code execution.

## Features of Python Turtle

### ✏️ Cursor as a Drawing Tool

The turtle acts as a pen or cursor controlled by user-defined commands. It draws shapes or patterns as it moves on the screen.

### ✏️ Directional Movement

The turtle can move forward, backward, left, and right, each defined with a specific length or angle.

### ✏️ Customizable Appearance

Users can change the turtle's color, shape, and size. Some predefined shapes include arrow, classic, square, triangle, and circle.

### ✏️ Drawing Geometric Shapes

By combining movement commands and loops, users can create polygons, fractals, spirals, and stars, among other complex patterns.

### ✏️ Animation Capabilities

Animations can be created by adjusting the speed, timing, and using loops to control the turtle's motion.

 

## Methods — Turtle

| | | | |
|---|---|---|---|
| done | goto | home | penup |
| mainloop | setx | undo | pendown |
| forward | sety | pencolor | teleport |
| fd | setheading | color | getshapes |
| backwards | seth | bgcolor | shape |
| bk | setpos | fillcolor | shapesize |
| right | setposition | begin_fill | hideturtle |
| rt | position | end_fill | hd |
| left | pos | pensize | showturtle |
| lt | clone | width | st |
| bye | write | stamp | speed |
| clear | reset | begin_poly | delay |
| clearscreen | resetscreen | end_poly | circle |
| title | exitonclick | bgpic | dots |
| tracer | clearstamp | pu | isdown |
| textinput | clearstamps | pd | isinvisible |
| back | numinput | up | turtlesize |
| distance | addshape | update | towards |

### Deep

To discover additional methods and attributes in the turtle module, use the dir() function

```
>>> import turtle
>>> tut = turtle.Turtle()
>>> dir(turtle)
```

### Note

After drawing shapes with Turtle, you can save everything on the screen as an **.eps** file using **getcanvas()** and **postscript(file)**. This .eps file can later be converted to an image. For example:

```
>>> from PIL import Image
>>> turtle.circle(100)
>>> tscreen = turtle.getscreen()
>>> tscreen.getcanvas().postscript(file = "shape.eps")
>>>
>>> img = Image.open("shape.eps")
>>> img.save("drawing.png")
```

 

# 1 Basic Turtle Operations

## done() and mainloop()

After drawing a shape, the screen normally closes immediately. The following methods prevent the screen from closing automatically after the drawing is completed:

- turtle.done(): Keeps the window open until manually closed.
- turtle.mainloop(): Similar to turtle.done(), keeps the turtle graphics window active.

```python
import turtle
turtle.done()
turtle.mainloop()
```

## bgcolor(color):

bgcolor() defines the background color of the turtle graphics window.
Colors can be specified in two formats:

- Named colors such as **"red"**, **"blue"**, **"purple"**, etc.
- Hexadecimal format **"#rrggbb"**, where **r**, **g**, and **b** are values from 0-9 or A-F.

```python
import turtle
turtle.bgcolor("#443E46")
turtle.mainloop()
```

# ❷ Movement and Positioning

### foward( float ) and fd( float )

Moves the turtle forward by the specified distance.

```python
import turtle
turtle.forward( 250 )
turtle.mainloop()
```

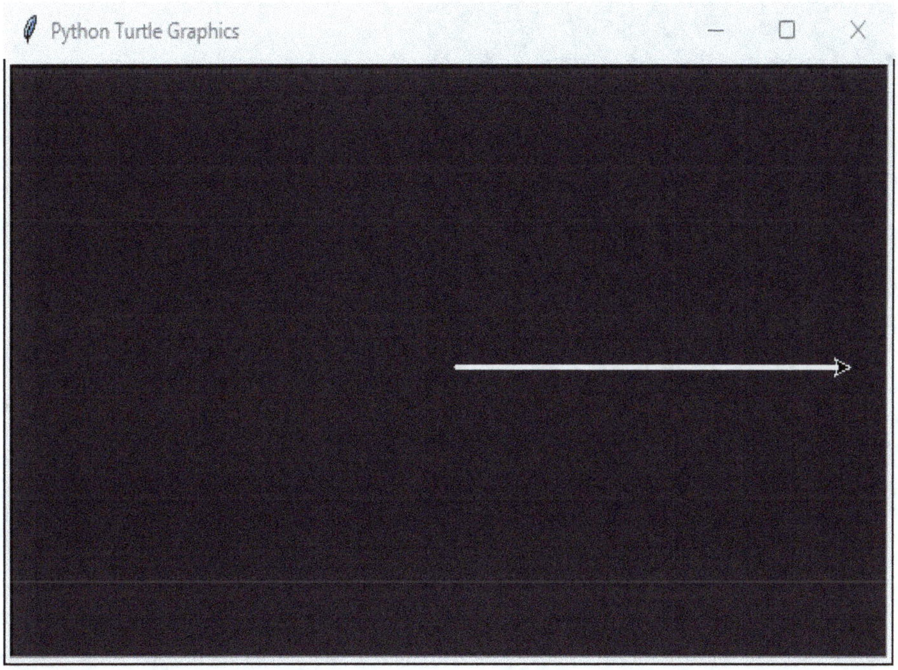


### backward( float ) and bk( float )

Moves the turtle backward by the specified distance.

```python
import turtle
turtle.bk( 100 )
turtle.mainloop()
```

 | 

### right( angle ) and rt( angle )

Rotates the turtle clockwise by the specified angle.

```
</> Python
import turtle
turtle.fd( 200 )
turtle.right( 90 )          #rotates by 90 degrees clockwise
turtle.fd( 200 )
turtle.mainloop()
```

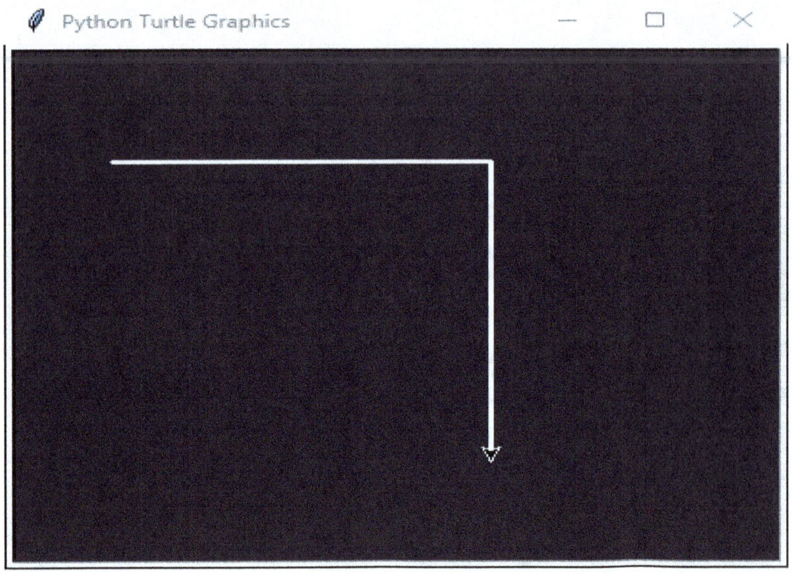


### left( angle ) and lt( angle )

Rotates the turtle counterclockwise by the specified angle.

```
</> Python
import turtle
turtle.forward( 200 )
turtle.left( 45 )          #rotates by 45 degrees counterclockwise
turtle.mainloop()
```

 

### goto( x, y )

Moves the turtle to the specified (x, y) coordinates.

```python
import turtle
turtle.goto( 50, 100 )        #moves turtle to 50 on x-axis and 100 on y-axis
turtle.goto( 100, 0 )
turtle.goto( 150, 0 )
turtle.goto( 200, 0 )
turtle.goto( 200, 0 )
turtle.goto( 150, -100 )
turtle.goto( 200, -200 )
turtle.goto( 50, -150 )
turtle.goto( 0, -200 )
turtle.mainloop()
```

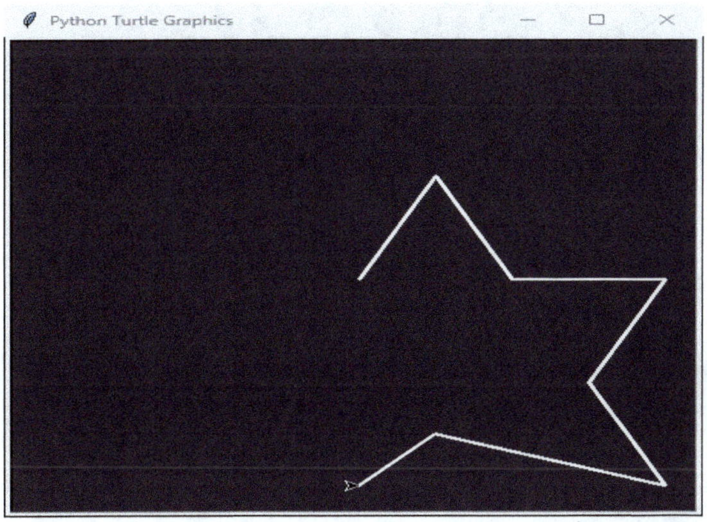


### setx( x ) and sety( y )

setx(x): Moves the turtle to a specific x-coordinate while keeping the y-coordinate constant.
sety(y): Moves the turtle to a specific y-coordinate while keeping the x-coordinate constant.

```python
import turtle
turtle.setx( 20 )     #set x coordinate to 20
turtle.sety( 45 )     #set y coordinate to 45
turtle.mainloop()
```

 

### setheading( angle ) and seth( angle )

Sets the turtle's heading to the specified angle.

```python
import turtle
turtle.forward( 100 )
turtle.setheading( 90 )       #turns to 90 degrees
turtle.forward( 50 )
turtle.done()
```

### setposition( x, y ) and setpos( x, y )

Moves the turtle to the specified (x, y) coordinates and begins drawing from that point.

```python
import turtle
turtle.setposition( 0, 100 )
turtle.setposition( 200, 100 )
turtle.setpos( 200, 0 )
turtle.setpos( 0, 0 )
turtle.done()
```

### position( ) and pos( )

Returns the current (x, y) coordinates of the turtle.

```python
import turtle
coord = turtle.position( )
print( coord )              #output : (0.00, 0.00)
```

 

**Think about it ?**

- clone(): Creates a duplicate instance of the turtle at the current position.
- home(): Moves the turtle to the origin (0,0) and resets the heading to 0 degrees.
- undo(): Removes the last action performed by the turtle, such as a drawn line.

## 3 Pen Control

pencolor( color ) and color( color )

These set the line color for drawing. It accepts:

- Named colors: **"red"**, **"green"**, **"blue"**, etc.
- Hexadecimal format **"#rrggbb"**, where **r**, **g**, and **b** are values from 0-9 or A-F.

</> **Python**

```
import turtle
turtle.color("orange")    #line color is set to red

for width in [200, 100, 200, 100]:
    turtle.forward( width )
    turtle.right( 90 )
turtle.done()
```

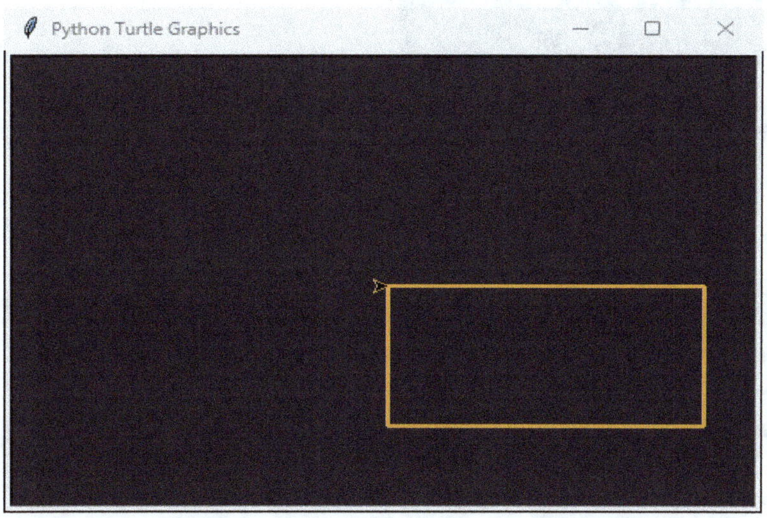


 

fillcolor( color ), begin_fill( color ) and .end_fill( color ),

The fillcolor defines the fill color for closed shapes.
begin_fill(): Marks the start of filling.
end_fill(): Completes and fills the drawn shape.
Colors can be specified in two formats:

- Named colors such as **"red"**, **"blue"**, **"purple"**, etc.
- Hexadecimal format **"#rrggbb"**, where **r**, **g**, and **b** are values from 0-9 or A-F.

</> Python

```
import turtle

tut = turtle.Turtle()
tut.fillcolor("#209010")    #fill color is set to green
tut.begin_fill()

for i in range( 4 ):
    tut.forward( 200 )
    tut.right( 90 )

tut.end_fill()
turtle.done()
```

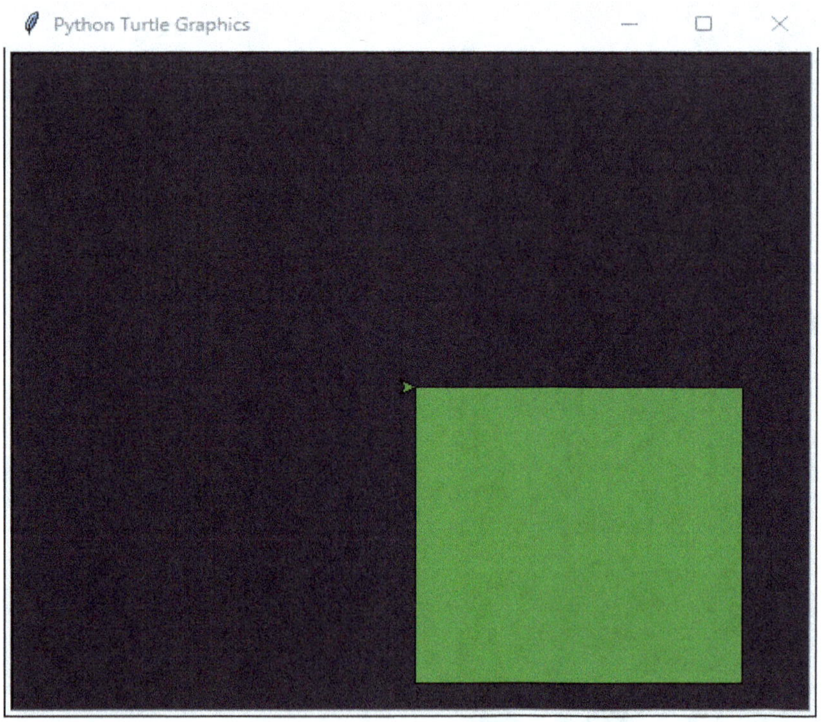


 

### penup( ) or pu( ) and pendown( ) or pd( )

turtle.penup() or turtle.pu() lifts the pen so the turtle moves without drawing.
turtle.pendown() or turtle.pd() lowers the pen so the turtle resumes drawing.

```python
import turtle

turtle.goto( 50, 100 )
turtle.goto( 100, 0 )
turtle.goto( 0, 0 )

turtle.penup( )
turtle.goto( -200, 0 )
turtle.pendown( )

for i in range( 4 ):
    turtle.forward( 100 )
    turtle.right( 90 )

turtle.done()
```

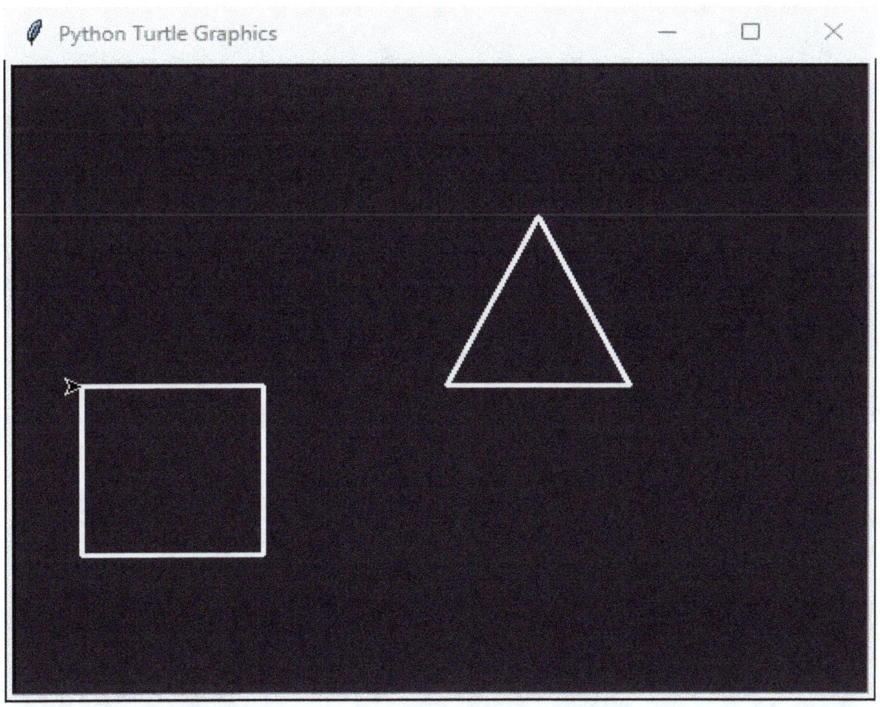


 

**Think about it ?**

📌 turtle.teleport(x, y):
Moves the turtle to a new position without drawing, similar to **penup()** and **pendown()** but with specified coordinates.

📌 What will the appearance be without using **penup()** and **pendown()**

pensize( float ) and width( float )

turtle.pensize(): Defines the thickness of the drawing line.
turtle.width(): Functions the same as pensize(), adjusting the pen thickness.

</> Python

```python
import turtle
turtle.pensize( 20 )
turtle.done()
```

# 4 Appearance and Shape Control

hideturtle( ) or ht( ) and showturtle( ) or st( )

The hideturtle() or ht() hides the turtle cursor from the screen.
The showturtle() or st() makes the turtle visible after hiding.

</> Python

```python
import turtle
turtle.showturtle( )
turtle.hideturtle( )
turtle.done()
```

 

### shape( shape ) , shapesize(stretch_wid, stretch_len, outline) and getshapes( )

The shape() sets the shape of the turtle cursor.
The shapesize() modifies the shape's width, length, and outline thickness.
The getshapes() returns a list of all available shapes. The following are available shapes.
"arrow", "blank", "circle", "classic", "square", "triangle", "turtle"

| Shape | Icon | Shape | Icon |
|---|---|---|---|
| arrow |  | triangle |  |
| square |  | turtle |  |
| circle |  | blank | |
| classic | 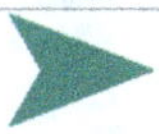 | | |

*Table 8.0: Some available turtle shapes*

</> Python

```python
import turtle
shapes = turtle.getshapes( )
print( shapes )            #output: ['arrow', 'blank', 'circle', 'classic', 'square', 'triangle', 'turtle']

turtle.shape("turtle" )
turtle.shapesize( stretch_wid= 10, stretch_len= 20,  outline = 2  )
```

### speed( int ) and delay( number )

The speed() sets the drawing speed from 0 (slowest) to 10 (fastest). Accepts strings: **"slow"**, **"normal"**, **"fast"**.
The delay() defines the time delay between turtle movements.

</> Python

```python
import turtle
turtle.speed( 5 )
turtle.delay(  3.5 )
turtle.done()
```

 | 

# 5 Drawing Shapes

circle( radius, extent=None, steps=None )

The circle() method allows the turtle to draw a circle with the specified radius.

extent → (float) [Optional]: Defines the length of the circumference to be drawn.

steps → (int) [Optional]: Specifies the number of points to form an enclosed polygon. Using steps, you can draw different polygons instead of a perfect circle.

</> **Python**

```python
import turtle
turtle.shape("turtle" )
turtle.color(  "purple", "orange")
turtle.begin_fill()
turtle.circle( radius = 100 )
turtle.end_fill()

turtle.mainloop()
```

**Think about it ?**

How can the **circle()** method be used to draw polygons?

 

```
</> Python
turtle.pensize( 5 )
turtle.shape( 'turtle' )
turtle.color("purple", "orange")
turtle.begin_fill()
turtle.circle(radius=100, steps= 3 )        #polygon with 3 sides (triangle)
turtle.teleport(x=-150, y= 100)
turtle.color("pink", "cyan")
turtle.circle(radius=100, steps= 4 )        #polygon with 4 sides (square)
turtle.teleport(x= 200, y= 50)
turtle.color("teal", "yellow")
turtle.circle(radius=100, steps= 5 )        #polygon with 5 sides (pentagon)
turtle.teleport(x= 50, y= -200)
turtle.color("red", "green")
turtle.circle(radius=100, steps= 6 )        #polygon with 6 sides (hexagon)
turtle.teleport(x= -150, y= -160)
turtle.color("purple", "orange")
turtle.circle(radius=100, steps= 7 )        #polygon with 7 size (heptagon)
turtle.end_fill()

turtle.mainloop()
```

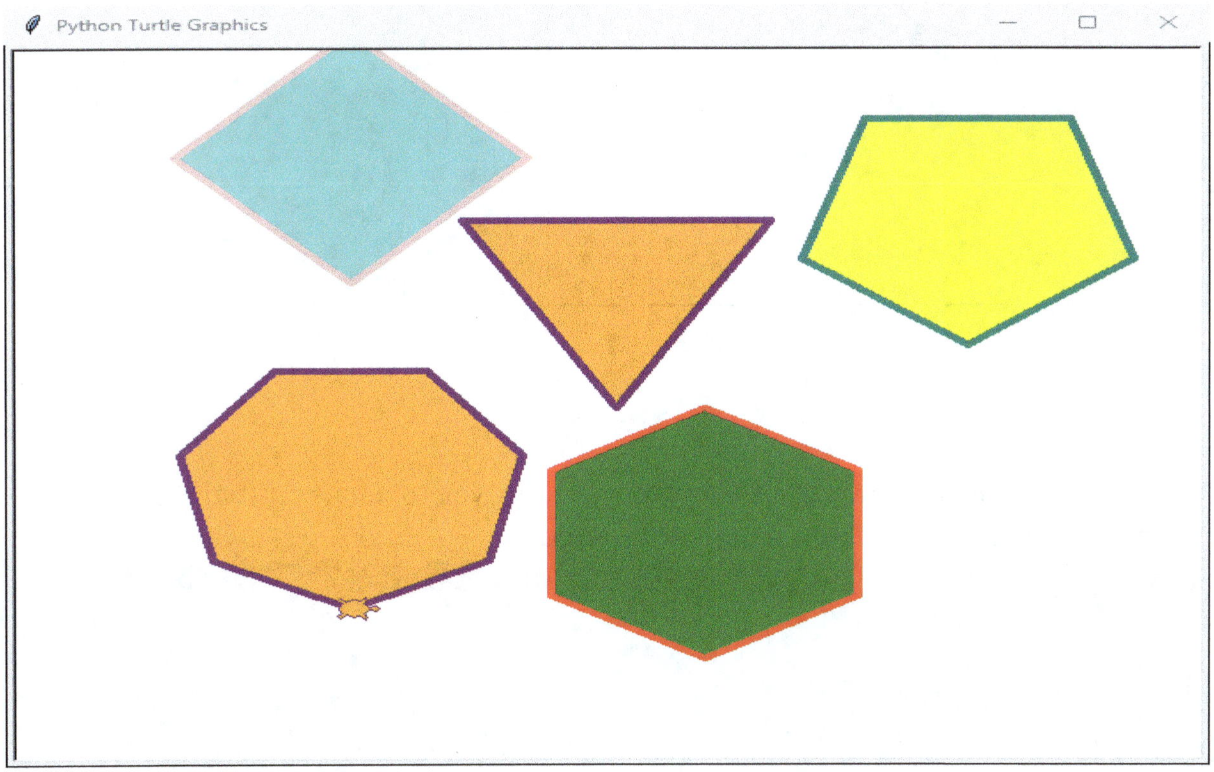


 

### dot( size)

The dot() method creates dots on the screen with a specified size (integer).

```python
import turtle
import random

colors = ["red", "orange", "green", "purple", "blue"]
for i in range(1, 500):
    turtle.pencolor(colors[random.randint(0,len(colors) -1)])
    turtle.dot(size=10)
    turtle.teleport(x=random.randint(-i, i), y=random.randint(-i, i))

turtle.mainloop()
```

### begin_poly( ) and end_poly( )

The begin_poly() marks the start of a polygon, allowing you to define custom shapes. The end_poly() marks the completion of the polygon.

```python
import turtle
turtle.begin_poly( )
turtle.end_poly( )
```

 

### write( arg, move, align, font )

The write() method prints text onto the screen with customizable options.

arg → Can be a string, number, list, dictionary, set, tuple, boolean, or bytes.

move → (bool) [Optional]: If True, the turtle moves by the length of the text. Default is False.

align → (string) [Optional]: Defines text alignment ("left", "center", or "right"). Default is "left".

font → (tuple) [Optional]: Defines the text appearance:

- Font Family (str) – Example: "Arial", "Consolas", "Times New Roman", "Tahoma", "Georgia".
- Font Size (int) – Defines the text size.
- Font Style (str) – "normal", "bold", "italic", or "underline".

</> Python

```
import turtle
turtle.bgcolor("orange")
turtle.color("white")
turtle.shape('turtle')
turtle.teleport(x=-30, y=50)
turtle.write(arg="Cracky Code", font=("tahoma", 25, "bold"))
turtle.teleport(x=-200, y=0)
turtle.write(arg="Awesome Python!☻", font=("Georgia", 30))
turtle.teleport(x=-30, y=-50)
turtle.write(arg="Just get me a coffee", align="center", font=("Georgia", 25, "italic"))
turtle.done()
```

**Think about it ?**

The **stamp()** method leaves an impression of the turtle's shape at its current position on the screen. Does it works the same way as the stamps used in letters?

# 6 Screen and Window Control

### bye( ), reset( ), cleaerscreen( ), and clear( )

The bye() closes the turtle window immediately.
The reset() resets the screen and clears all drawings.
The clearscreen() clears all shapes drawn by the turtle.
The clear() clears only the currently drawn object.

```python
import turtle
turtle.bye( )
turtle.reset( )
turtle.clearscreen( )
turtle.clear( )
```

### title( title ) and exitonclick()

The title() sets the window title.
The exitonclick() closes the window when clicked.

```python
import turtle
turtle.title( "My Title" )
turtle.exitonclick( )
```

 

# Examples of Shapes Created Using Turtle

1. Flower with Spiral Petals

```python
import turtle
import math

t = turtle.Turtle()
t.speed(0)
turtle.bgcolor("#F5F8FA")
t.pensize(1)
t.pencolor("red")

# Function to draw a spiral flower
def flower(petals, angle_step, size_factor):
    for i in range(petals):
        t.forward(math.sqrt(i) * size_factor)
        t.left(angle_step)

# Draw the flower
flower(360, 65, 10)

turtle.done()
```

```python
import turtle
import math

t = turtle.Turtle()
t.speed(0)
turtle.bgcolor("#F5F8FA")
t.pensize(1)
t.pencolor("purple")

# Function to draw a spiral flower
def flower(petals, angle_step, size_factor):
    for i in range(petals):
        t.forward(math.sqrt(i) * size_factor)
        t.left(angle_step)

# Draw the flower
flower(360, 100, 20)

turtle.done()
```

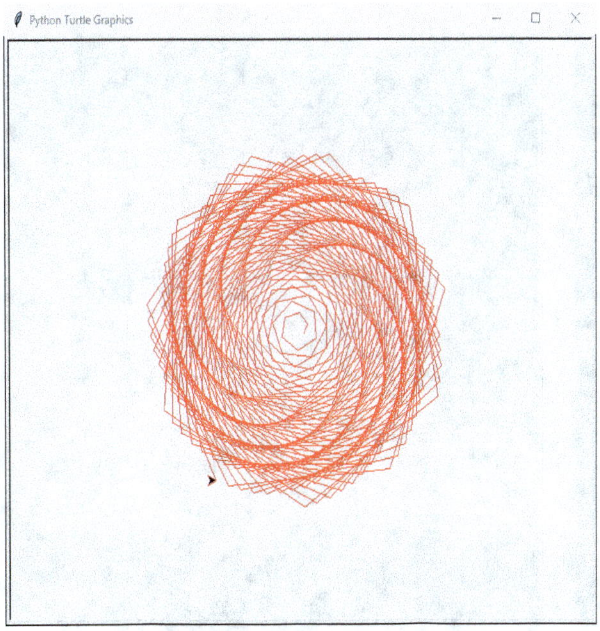


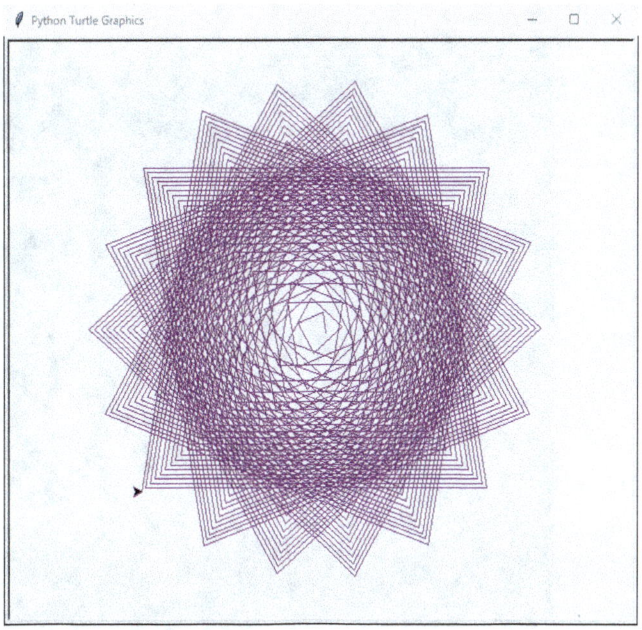


 

2. Colorful spiral flower

```python
import turtle
import random

t = turtle.Turtle()
t.speed(0)
turtle.bgcolor("#14171A")
t.pensize(1)
colors = ["red","yellow","green","blue","orange","purple"]

# Function to draw a spiral flower
def flower(petals, angle_step):
    for i in range(petals):
        t.pencolor(random.choice(colors))
        t.forward( i )
        t.left(angle_step)

# Draw the flower
flower(360, 59)

turtle.done()
```

```python
import turtle
import random

t = turtle.Turtle()
t.speed(0)
turtle.bgcolor("#14171A")
colors = ["red","yellow","green","blue","orange","purple"]

# Function to draw a spiral flower
def flower(petals, size, angle):
    for i in range(petals):
        t.pencolor(random.choice(colors))
        t.circle( size )
        t.left(angle)

# Draw the flower
flower( 72, 100, 10)

turtle.done()
```

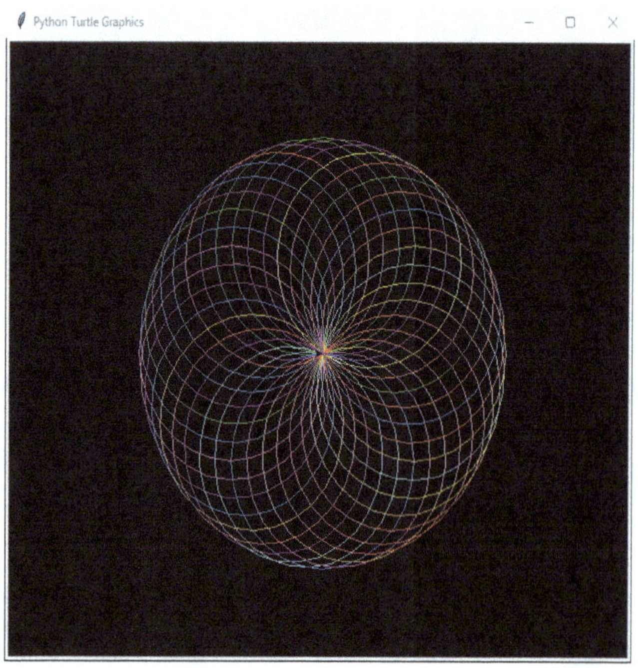


 

2. Colorful square flower

```
import turtle
import random

t = turtle.Turtle()
t.speed(0)
turtle.bgcolor("#14171A")
colors = ["red","yellow","green","blue","orange","purple"]

def create_square(size):
    for i in range(4):
        t.forward( size )
        t.right(90)

def flower(repeat, size, angle):
    for i in range(repeats):
        t.pencolor(random.choice(colors))
        create_square(size )
        t.right(angle)

flower(72, 100, 10)
turtle.done()
```

```
import turtle

t = turtle.Turtle()
t.speed(0)
turtle.bgcolor("#14171A")
colors = ["red","yellow","green","blue","orange","purple"]


for i in range( 100 ):
    t.pencolor( colors[ i % len(colors)])
    t.forward( i * 5 )
    t.right( 91 )

turtle.done()
```

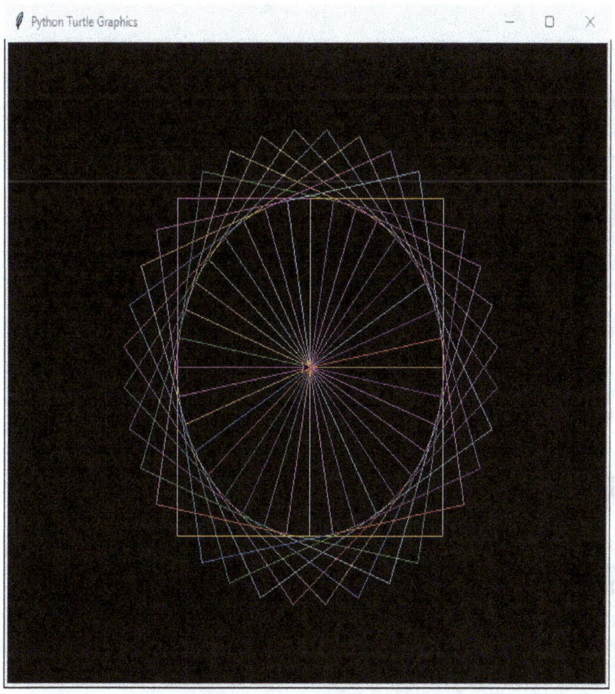


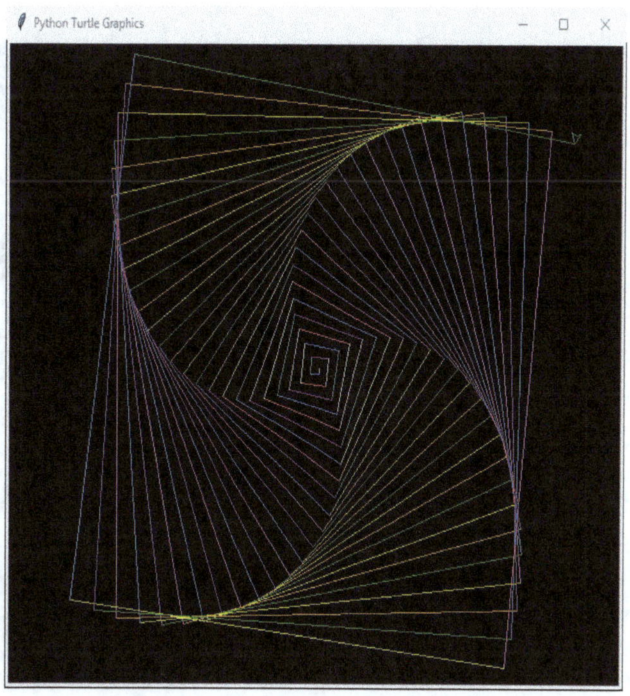


 

2. Colorful hexagonal flower

```python
import turtle

t = turtle.Turtle()
t.speed(0)
turtle.bgcolor("#14171A")
colors = ["red","yellow","green","blue","orange","purple"]

for i in range( 6 ):
    t.pencolor( colors[ i % len(colors)])
    for _ in range( 6 ):
        t.forward( 100 )
        t.right( 60 )
    t.right( 60 )


turtle.done()
```

```python
import turtle

t = turtle.Turtle()
t.speed(0)
turtle.bgcolor("#ffffff")


for i in range( 100 ):
    for _ in range( 3 ):
        t.forward( i * 4 )
        t.right( 140 )
    t.right( 5 )


turtle.done()
```

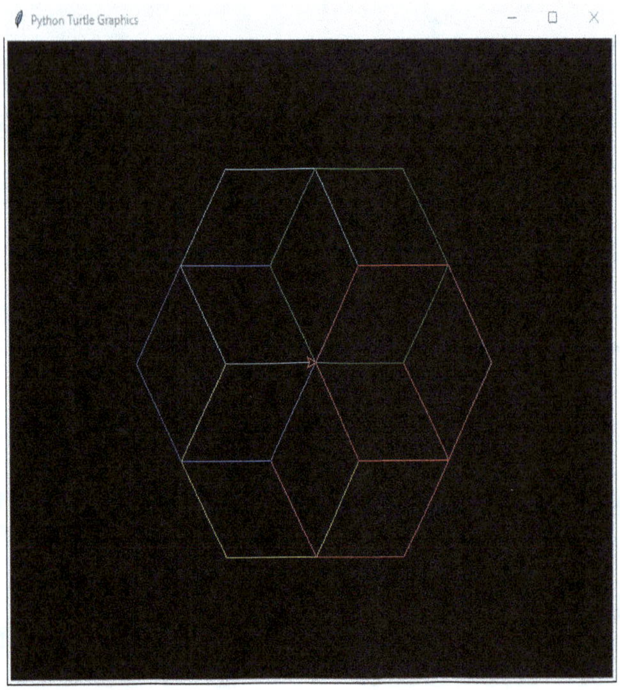

# Chapter Summary

Python's turtle module is a built-in library used for drawing shapes on the screen. It is designed to make learning Python more engaging by providing a graphical way to explore programming concepts.

The name *turtle* comes from the idea of a small turtle moving in different directions to draw shapes on the screen. With turtle, you can create both simple and complex designs, depending on your level of coding skills.

To keep the turtle graphics window open after execution, the mainloop() or done() function must be used.

The turtle module includes various methods for controlling movement and drawing, such as:

- forward(), backward(), right(), left(), and circle() to control direction and motion.
- shape() to change the appearance of the turtle. Available shapes include "circle", "square", "turtle", "triangle", "blank", "arrow", and "classic".
- pensize(size) to adjust the pointer thickness, pencolor(color) to change the pen color, and fillcolor(color) to set the fill color of a shape.
- speed(value) to control drawing speed.

To reposition the turtle without drawing, use penup() (or pu()), and to resume drawing, use pendown() (or pd()). The getshapes() method allows you to check all available turtle shapes.

Besides drawing, turtle can also write text on the screen using the write() method and accept user input via a dialog box with textinput().

## Key Terms

animation    stamp    polygon    clockwise

counterclockwise    classic    coordinate

## Discussion

1. How does Python's turtle module make programming more interactive and engaging for beginners?
2. What are the key differences between forward(), backward(), right(), and left() in the turtle module? How can they be combined to draw complex shapes?
3. How does the shape() method change the turtle's appearance? What are some creative ways to use different shapes in a drawing?
4. How do penup() and pendown() impact the drawing process? In what scenarios would you use them?
5. How can the textinput() method be used to make an interactive drawing application with turtle? What are some practical applications of this feature?
6. Why is the mainloop() or done() method necessary when working with turtle? What happens if you forget to include it in your script?
7. How can you customize the turtle's drawing using pencolor(), fillcolor(), and pensize()? Can you combine these methods to create artistic effects?
8. How does the speed() method affect the animation of turtle drawings? In what situations would adjusting the speed be useful?

# Review Questions

1. Choose the methods with the same functionality:
a. turtle.forward() and turtle.backward()
b. turtle.right() and turtle.bk()
c. turtle.backward() and turtle.fd()
d. turtle.fd() and turtle.forward()

2. What is the best way to prevent drawing while moving the turtle to a different position?
a. turtle.penup() and turtle.right()
b. turtle.pu() and turtle.penup()
c. turtle.pd() and turtle.penup()
d. turtle.pendown() and turtle.pd()

3. Choose the correct sequence to create the given shape:

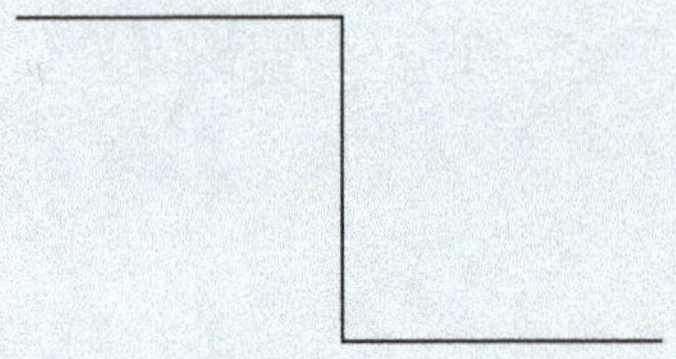

a. turtle.forward(50), turtle.right(90), turtle.forward(50), turtle.right(90), turtle.forward(50),
b. turtle.backward(50), turtle.right(90), turtle.forward(50), turtle.right(90), turtle.forward(50)
c. turtle.left(90), turtle.backward(50), turtle.right(90), turtle.forward(50)
d. turtle.forward(100), turtle.right(90), turtle.forward(50), turtle.left(90), turtle.forward(50),

4. Which shape does the turtle draw with the following movements?

```
turtle.right(45)
turtle.forward(150)
turtle.right(135)
turtle.forward(200)
turtle.right(135)
turtle.forward(150)
```

a. Square
b. Triangle
c. Rectangle
d. Rhombus

5. Which of the following is **not** a valid turtle shape?
a. Classic
b. Oval
c. Turtle
d. Square

6. Which method prevents the screen from closing immediately after drawing?
a. clone()
b. mainloop()
c. time()
d. pen()

7. Which method combines the functionality of both penup() and pendown()?
a. teleport()
b. pd()
c. setpos()
d. deepcopy()

8. What is the default turtle shape?
a. Circle
b. Classic
c. Turtle
d. Arrow

9. Choose the correct way to use the color() method
a. turtle.color(red)
b. turtle.color = "red"
c. turtle.color("red")
d. turtle.color() = red

10. What does the undo() method do?
a. Clears the entire screen
b. Deletes the first line drawn
c. Deletes the last line drawn
d. Clears the current figure

# Remarks

Thank you so much for taking the time to read this book. I sincerely appreciate your support, and I pray that the Almighty God replenishes every penny you have spent on this book. May you be blessed abundantly.

Ouereila Publishing House is continuously growing, and we acknowledge that we are not yet perfect. Your feedback is invaluable in helping us improve and refine our work. If you have any suggestions, comments, or insights, please feel free to share them with us at ouereila@gmail.com or through this feedback form. Your input will contribute to the betterment of not only this book but also future publications.


# Acknowledgment

First and foremost, I extend my deepest gratitude to the Almighty God for guiding me through this journey and giving me the strength to complete this work.

A special thanks goes to my dear mother, **Irene**, for her unwavering love, encouragement, and belief in me. Her support has been a cornerstone of my journey, and I pray she continues to live a long and fulfilling life.

Additionally, I extend my gratitude to everyone who has supported me in any way—whether through words of encouragement, constructive feedback, or simply believing in this vision. Your contributions, big or small, have played a role in bringing this book to life.

May this book serve as a stepping stone for those eager to explore the world of Python graphics.

With appreciation,
**Williams Asiedu**


 

# About the Author

Williams Asiedu is a software engineer, entrepreneur, and philanthropist. He earned his Master's degree from the Illinois Institute of Technology and currently works as a software engineer.

Beyond his work in software development, Williams is also a publisher and author, with multiple books to his name. He has written extensively on computer science and programming and has also collaborated with other authors to contribute to the field.

As a philanthropist, Williams is deeply committed to giving back to society. His generosity and dedication to community development have positively impacted many lives. Through his work, he continues to inspire and support aspiring technologists and innovators.

 

www.ingramcontent.com/pod-product-compliance
Lightning Source LLC
LaVergne TN
LVHW080048210926
848481LV00011B/3300
* 9 7 9 8 3 4 9 3 9 0 6 9 2 *